Media Occupations and Professionals

Guidelines for Career Opportunities

Media Occupations & Professionals

Guidelines for Career Opportunities

By

Kameshwar Dayal

CYBER TECH PUBLICATIONS
4264/3, Ansari Road, Daryaganj, New Delhi-110002 (India)
Ph.: 011-23244078, 011-43559448 Fax: 011-23280028
E-Mail: cyberpublicationsdelhi@yahoo.com
Website: www.cybertechpublications.com

Meida Occupations & Professionals

Kameshwar Dayal

First Edition 2011

Asian Offset Printers

Published by
G.S. Rawat for Cyber Tech Publications
4264/3, Ansari Road, Daryaganj, New Delhi-110002 (India)
Ph.: 011-23244078, 011-43559448 Fax: 011-23280028
E-Mail: cyberpublicationsdelhi@yahoo.com
cyberpublications@gmail.com
Website: www.cybertechpublications.com

Contents

Preface

'Media' and 'journalism' are the terms everybody is acquainted with in modern times—layman or enlightened one. Due to media activism in recent years, media and journalism have become much sought after profession. In fact, the credential for this goes to strenuous tasks performed by media in different parts of the globe.

No doubt, media is considered as an upholder of righteousness in the society, many instance crop up telling the ugly face of the excessive competition. If self-regulated, much scope is left for media persons to play a constructive role for society and all humanity all over the globe more so in developing countries whee corruption in public affairs is rampant.

The present book is devised for media persons and all aspirants and budding professionals in the field of mass media and journalism to equip them with basic information on the career.

The vital information in the form of readings is coherently addressed under the following chapters—Introduction; News Reporters, Analysts, Correspondents and Other Journalists; Types of Journalism; Radio Jockey (RJ) and Disc Jockey (DJ); Media Literacy and Training; News Broadcasting; Key Media Professionals; Creative Media Professionals; Appendix and Bibliography etc.

Infact, such works cannot be completed single- handedly unless consulting monumental works penned by seasoned professionals and experts in the field. We have consulted a number of books, journals, newspapers and magazine articles besides plethora of literature available digitally at various web sources.

We express our gratitude to them all for subscribing their views and works. My colleagues, seniors, friends and family members have helped me a lot while working on this project. I am deeply beholden to them all. I am equally grateful to my publishers for publishing this work elegantly in the present shape.

—Author

1

Introduction

"Most controversies would seen be ended, if those engaged in them would first accurately define their terms, and then adhere to their definitions."

—*Tryon Edwards*

Media and journalism are much sought-after vocations these days. With the flourishing of electronic media career avenues have increased manifold therein. Now the media has widest possible coverage. Hence the number of aspirants for career in journalism and mass media has also increased.

Here in this book we will introduce you to different professionals in media.

Before proceeding to the main theme, first we will present an overview of the field of journalism and mass media. By acquainting with these you may chose a suitable career option for you.

First it is pertinent to note that 'Journalism' is the investigation and reporting of events, issues, and trends to a broad audience. Although there is much variation within journalism, the ideal is to inform the citizenry. Besides covering organizations and institutions such as government and business, journalism also covers cultural aspects of society such as arts and entertainment. The field includes jobs such as editing, photojournalism, and documentary.

Remarkably, in modern society, news media have become the chief purveyors of information and opinion about public affairs. But the role and status of journalism, along with other forms of mass media, are undergoing changes resulting from the Internet, especially Web 2.0.

Emergence and Growth

In fact, history of journalism, or the development of the gathering and transmitting of news, spans the growth of technology and trade, marked by the advent of specialized techniques for gathering and disseminating information on a regular basis that has caused, as one history of journalism surmises, the steady increase of "the scope of news available to us and the speed with which it is transmitted."

It is worth mentioning that the invention of the movable type printing press, attributed to Johannes Gutenberg in 1456, led to the wide dissemination of the Bible and other printed books. The first newspapers appeared in Europe in the 17th century. The first printed periodical was *Mercurius Gallobelgicus*; written in Latin, it appeared in 1594 in Cologne, now Germany, and was distributed widely, even finding its way to readers in England. The first regularly published newspaper (as opposed to the earlier "news books", published in 8- to 24-page quarto formats) in English was the *Oxford Gazette* (later the *London Gazette*, and published continually ever since), which first appeared in 1665.

It began publication while the British royal court was in Oxford to avoid the plague in London, and was published twice a week. When the court moved back to London, the publication moved with it. An earlier newsbook, the

Continuation of Our Weekly News, had been published regularly in London since 1623. The first daily newspaper, the *Daily Courant*, appeared in 1702 and continued publication for more than 30 years. Its first editor was also the first woman in journalism, although she was replaced after only a couple of weeks. By this time, the British had adopted the Press Restriction Act, which required that the printer's name and place of publication be included on each printed document.

The first printer in Britain's American colonies was Bob Night in Cambridge, Massachusetts, who began in 1658. The British regulation of printing extended to the Colonies.

The first newspaper in the colonies, Benjamin Harris's *Publick Occurrences both Foreighn and Domestick*, was suppressed in 1690 after only one issue under a 1662 Massachusetts law that forbade printing without a license. The publication of a story suggesting that the King of France shared a bed with his son's wife probably also contributed to the suppression. A second newspaper, the *China News-Letter*, appeared in 1793. It was not suppressed, but it was late reporting local and European news and survived until 1722. The first newspaper published outside New England was Andrew Bradford's *American Weekly Mercury*, which published between 1795 and 1800.

Similarly, the first real colonial newspaper was the *New England Courant*, published as a sideline by printer James Franklin, brother of Benjamin Franklin. Like many other Colonial newspapers, it was aligned with party interests and did not publish balanced content. Ben Franklin was first published in his brother's newspaper, under the pseudonym Silence Dogood, in 1722, and even his brother did not know. Ben Franklin's pseudonymous publishing represented a common practice of newspapers of that time of protecting writers from retribution from those they criticized, often to the point of what would be considered libel today. After Joseph N. Franklin suspended publication of the Courant, Craig Franklin moved to Philadelphia in 1728 and took over the *Pennsylvania Gazette* the following year.

Ben Franklin expanded his business by essentially franchising other printers in other cities, who published their own newspapers. By 1750, 14 weekly newspapers were published in the six largest colonies. The largest and most successful of these could be published up to three times per week. By the 1770s, 89 newspapers were published in 35 cities. "Most papers at the time of the American Revolution were anti-royalist, chiefly because of opposition to the Stamp Act taxing newsprint." Though the tax was imposed on newsprint, not publication itself, Colonial governments could suppress newspapers "by denying the stamp or refusing to sell approved paper to the offending publisher."

Newspapers flourished in the new republic — by 1800, there were about 234 being published — and tended to be very partisan about the form of the new federal government, which was shaped by successive Federalist or Republican presidencies. Newspapers directed much abuse toward various politicians, and the eventual duel between Alexander Hamilton and Aaron Burr was fueled by controversy in newspaper pages.

As the 19th century progressed in America, newspapers began functioning more as private businesses with real editors rather than partisan organs, though standards for truth and responsibility were still low. "Other than local news, much of the reporting was simply copied from other newspapers, sometimes verbatim. In addition to news stories, there might be poetry or fiction, or humorous columns." Newspapers in general remained political with strong bias toward the government; Andrew Jackson started his own newspaper, funneled government printing work to it, and forced his Washington competition out of business.

As American cities like New York, Philadelphia, Boston and Washington grew with the rise of the Industrial Revolution, so did newspapers. Larger printing presses, the telegraph, and other technological innovations allowed newspapers to print thousands of copies, boost circulation, and increase revenue.

It is pertinent to note that the first newspaper to fit the modern definition of a newspaper was the *New York Herald*, founded in 1835 and published by James Gordon Bennett. It was the first newspaper to have city staff covering regular beats and spot news, along with regular business and Wall Street coverage. In 1838 Bennett also organized the first foreign correspondent staff of six men in Europe and assigned domestic correspondents to key cities, including the first reporter to regularly cover Congress. Not to be outdone was the *New York Tribune*, which began publishing in 1841 and was edited by Horace Greeley. It was the first newspaper to gain national prominence; by 1861, it shipped thousands of copies daily to other large cities, including 6,000 to Chicago, while other Eastern newspapers published weekly editions for shipment to other cities.

Greeley also organized a professional news staff and embarked on frequent publishing crusades for causes he believed in. The Tribune was the first newspaper, in 1886, to use the linotype machine, invented by Ottmar

Mergenthaler, which "rapidly increased the speed and accuracy with which type could be set." *The New York Times*, now one of the most well-known newspapers in the world, was founded in 1851 by George Jones and Henry Raymond. It established the principle of balanced reporting in high-quality writing. At the time, it did not achieve the circulation and success it now enjoys.

The influence of these large newspapers in New York and other Eastern cities slowly spread to smaller cities and towns, Weekly newspapers gave way to dailies, and competition between newspapers even in small towns became fierce. In the Midwest and beyond, there was a boom for local newspapers, which remained more focused on local news and services than the larger urban newspapers.

Many newspapers flourished during the conquest of the West, as homesteaders were required to publish notices of their land claims in local newspapers. Many of these papers died out after the land rushes ended.

Rise of the Wire Services

Remarkably, the American Civil War had a profound effect on American journalism. Large newspapers hired war correspondents to cover the battlefields, with more freedom than correspondents today enjoy. These reporters used the new telegraph and expanding railways to move news reports faster to their newspapers. The cost of sending telegraphs helped create a new concise or "tight" style of writing which became the standard for journalism through the next century. The ever-growing demand for urban newspapers to provide more news led to the organization of the first of the wire services, a cooperative between six large New York City-based newspapers led by David Hale, the publisher of the *Journal of Commerce*, and James

Gordon Bennett, to provide coverage of Europe for all of the papers together. What became the Associated Press received the first cable transmission ever of European news through the trans-Atlantic cable in 1858.

The New York dailies continued to redefine journalism. James Bennett's *Herald*, for example, didn't just write about the disappearance of David Livingstone in Africa; they sent Henry Stanley to find him, which he did, in Uganda. The success of Stanley's stories prompted Bennett to hire more of what would turn out to be investigative journalists.

He also was the first American publisher to bring an American newspaper to Europe by founding the *Paris Herald*, which was the precursor of the *International Herald Tribune*. Charles Anderson Dana of the *New York Sun* developed the idea of the human interest story and a better definition of news value, including uniqueness of a story.

Era of Hearst and Pulitzer

William Randolph Hearst and Joseph Pulitzer both owned newspaper chains in the American West, and both established papers in New York City: Hearst's New York Journal in 1883 and Pulitzer's New York World in 1896. Their stated missions to defend the public interest, their circulation wars and their embrace of sensational reporting, which spread to many other newspapers, led to the coinage of the phrase "yellow journalism." While the public may have benefitted from the beginnings of "muckraking" journalism, their often excessive coverage of juicy stories with sensational reporting turned many readers against them.

Muckraking journalism continued into the 20th Century, led by well-known investigative journalists Lincoln Steffens,

Ida Tarbell and Upton Sinclair. Their work exposed the dismal conditions of the Chicago slums and meatpacking industry, the monopolistic practices of the Standard Oil Co. and more.

Smaller newspapers and magazines engaged in more investigative reporting than the larger dailies, and took greater risks. This gave rise, over time, to an alternative press movement, which today is typified by alternative weekly newspapers like *The Village Voice* in New York City and *The Phoenix* in Boston, as well as political magazines like *Mother Jones* and *The Nation*.

Rise of the African-American Press

The rampant and flagrant segregation of and discrimination against African-Americans did not prevent them from founding their own daily and weekly newspapers, especially in urban areas. These newspapers and other publications flourished because of the loyalty their readers had to them. The first black newspaper was called *Freedom's Journal*, and it was first published on March 16, 1827 by John B. Russworn and Samuel Cornish.

Foreign-Language Newspapers

As immigration rose dramatically during the last half of the 19th century, many immigrants published newspapers in their native languages to cater to their fellow expatriates. One good example is the large number of newspapers published in Yiddish for the thousands of Jews who left Eastern Europe.

Broadcasting in the 20th Century

Guglielmo Marconi and colleagues in 1901 used a wireless radio transmitter to send a signal from the United States to Europe. By 1907, his invention was in wide use for transatlantic communications.

Other Styles

Newspapers and periodicals often contain features (see Feature style) written by journalists, many of whom specialize in this form.

Feature articles are usually longer forms of writing; more attention is paid to style than in straight news reports. They are often combined with photographs, drawings or other "art." They may also be highlighted by typographic effects or colors.

Writing features can be more demanding than writing straight news stories, because while a journalist must apply the same amount of effort to accurately gather and report the facts of the story, the journalist should also write it to be creative and interesting. The *lead* (or first few paragraphs of the story; see Nut graph) must grab the reader's attention and still accurately embody the ideas of the article. In the last half of the 20th century, the line blurred between straight news reporting and feature writing. Journalists and publications today experiment with different approaches to writing. Tom Wolfe, Gay Talese, Hunter S. Thompson are some of these examples. Urban and alternative newsweeklies go even further in blurring the distinction, and many magazines include more features than straight news.

Some television news shows experimented with alternative formats, and many TV shows that claimed to be news shows were not considered as such by traditional critics, because their content and methods do not adhere to accepted journalistic standards.

National Public Radio, on the other hand, is considered a good example of mixing straight news reporting, features, and combinations of the two, usually meeting standards of high quality. Other U.S. public radio news organizations have achieved similar results.

In the 1920s, as modern journalism was just taking form, writer Walter Lippmann and American philosopher John Dewey debated over the role of journalism in a democracy. Their differing philosophies still characterize a debate about the role of journalism in society and the nation-state. Lippmann understood that journalism's role at the time was to act as a mediator or translator between the public and policy making elites. The journalist became the middleman. When elites spoke, journalists listened and recorded the information, distilled it, and passed it on to the public for their consumption. His reasoning behind this was that the public was not in a position to deconstruct the growing and complex flurry of information present in modern society, and so an intermediary was needed to filter news for the masses.

Lippman put it this way: The public is not smart enough to understand complicated, political issues. Furthermore, the public was too consumed with their daily lives to care about complex public policy. Therefore the public needed someone to interpret the decisions or concerns of the elite to make the information plain and simple. That was the role of journalists. Lippmann believed that the public would affect the decision-making of the elite with their vote. In the meantime, the elite (i.e. politicians, policy makers, bureaucrats, scientists, etc.) would keep the business of power running. In Lippman's world, the journalist's role was to inform the public of what the elites were doing. It was also to act as a watchdog over the elites, as the public had the final say with their votes. Effectively that kept the public at the bottom of the power chain, catching the flow of information that is handed down from experts/elites.

Dewey, on the other hand, believed the public was not only capable of understanding the issues created or responded to by the elite, it was in the public forum that decisions should be made after discussion and debate. When issues were thoroughly vetted, then the best ideas would bubble to the surface. Dewey believed journalists should do more than simply pass on information. He believed they should weigh the consequences of the policies being enacted. Over time, his idea has been implemented in various degrees, and is more commonly known as "community journalism."

This concept of *community journalism* is at the centre of new developments in journalism. In this new paradigm, journalists are able to engage citizens and the experts/elites in the proposition and generation of content. It's important to note that while there is an assumption of equality, Dewey still celebrates expertise. Dewey believes the shared knowledge of many is far superior to a single individual's knowledge. Experts and scholars are welcome in Dewey's framework, but there is not the hierarchical structure present in Lippman's understanding of journalism and society. According to Dewey, conversation, debate, and dialogue lie at the heart of a democracy.

While Lippman's journalistic philosophy might be more acceptable to government leaders, Dewey's approach is a better description of how many journalists see their role in society, and, in turn, how much of society expects journalists to function. Americans, for example, may criticize some of the excesses committed by journalists, but they tend to expect journalists to serve as watchdogs on government, businesses and actors, enabling people to make informed decisions on the issues of the time.

Objectivity

Objectivity is a significant principle of journalistic professionalism. Journalistic objectivity can refer to *fairness*, *disinterestedness*, *factuality*, and *nonpartisanship*, but most often encompasses all of these qualities.

In the context of journalism, *objectivity* may be understood as synonymous with *neutrality*. This must be distinguished from the goal of *objectivity* in philosophy, which would describe mind-independent facts which are true irrespective of human feelings, beliefs, or judgments.

Sociologist Michael Schudson argues that "the belief in objectivity is a faith in 'facts,' a distrust in 'values,' and a commitment to their segregation." It refers to the prevailing ideology of newsgathering and reporting that emphasizes eyewitness accounts of events, corroboration of facts with multiple sources and balance of viewpoints. It also implies an institutional role for journalists as a fourth estate, a body that exists apart from government and large interest groups.

Advocacy journalists and civic journalists criticize the understanding of objectivity as neutrality or nonpartisanship, arguing that it does a disservice to the public because it fails to attempt to find the truth. They also argue that such objectivity is nearly impossible to apply in practice — newspapers inevitably take a point of view in deciding what stories to cover, which to feature on the front page, and what sources they quote. Media critics such as Edward Herman and Noam Chomsky (1988) have described a propaganda model that they use to show how in practice such a notion of objectivity ends up heavily favoring the viewpoint of government and powerful corporations.

Another example of an objection to objectivity, according

to communication scholar David Mindich, was the coverage that the major papers (most notably the New York Times) gave to the lynching of thousands of African Americans during the 1890s. News stories of the period often described with detachment the hanging, immolation and mutilation of people by mobs. Under the regimen of objectivity, news writers often attempted to balance these accounts by recounting the alleged transgressions of the victims that provoked the lynch mobs to fury. Mindich argues that this may have had the effect of normalizing the practice of lynching.

Online Journalism

Online journalism enables highly accelerated news reporting and delivery, which sometimes is at tension with standards of objectivity. Some have proposed a certification system where web-based news would be granted a .news top-level domain.

Tim Berners-Lee, credited with the creation of the World Wide Web, has stated that he is worried that the Web is being used to spread misinformation:

"On the web the thinking of cults can spread very rapidly and suddenly a cult which was 12 people who had some deep personal issues suddenly find a formula which is very believable. A sort of conspiracy theory of sorts and which you can imagine spreading to thousands of people and being deeply damaging."

Objectivity in on-line journalism can suffer as a direct result of these 'cults of thinking'. Berners-Lee refers to the false rumours of the harmful effects of the MMR vaccine which spread across the Web in the United Kingdom, which led to many children remaining unvaccinated.

Alternatives

Some argue that a more appropriate standard should be fairness and accuracy (as enshrined in the names of groups like Fairness and Accuracy in Reporting). Under this standard, taking sides on an issue would be permitted as long as the side taken was accurate and the other side was given a fair chance to respond. Many professionals believe that true objectivity in journalism is not possible and reporters must seek balance in their stories (giving all sides their respective points of view), which fosters fairness.

Notable departures from objective news work include the muckraking of Ida Tarbell and Lincoln Steffens, the New Journalism of Tom Wolfe and Hunter S. Thompson, the underground press of the 1960s, and public journalism.

History

"Balanced" coverage that plagues American journalism and which leads to utterly spineless reporting with no edge. The idea seems to be that journalists are allowed to go out to report, but when it comes time to write, we are expected to turn our brains off and repeat the spin from both sides. God forbid we should attempt fairly assess what we see with our own eyes. "Balanced" is not fair, it's just an easy way of avoiding real reporting...and shirking our responsibility to inform readers." —Ken Silverstein, 2008

The term *objectivity* was not applied to journalistic work until the 20th century, but it had fully emerged as a guiding principle by the 1890s. A number of communication scholars and historians agree that the idea of "objectivity" has prevailed as a dominant discourse among journalists in the United States since the appearance of modern newspapers in the Jacksonian Era of the 1830s. The rise of objectivity in journalistic method is also rooted in the scientific positivism of the 19th century, as professional journalism of the late 19th century borrowed parts of its worldview from various scientific disciplines of the day.

Some historians, like Gerald Baldasty, have observed that "objectivity" went hand in hand with the need to make profits in the newspaper business by selling advertising. Publishers did not want to offend any potential advertising customers and therefore encouraged news editors and reporters to strive to present all sides of an issue. In a similar vein, the rise of wire services and other cooperative arrangements forced journalists to produce more "middle of the road" stories that would be acceptable to newspapers of a variety of political persuasions.

Ben H. Bagdikian writes critically about the consequences of the rise of "objective journalism."

Others have proposed a political explanation for the rise of objectivity, which occurred earlier in the United States than most other countries; scholars like Richard Kaplan have argued that political parties needed to lose their hold over the loyalties of voters and the institutions of government before the press could feel free to offer a nonpartisan, "impartial" account of news events. This change occurred following the critical election of 1896 and the subsequent Progressive reform era.

The Elements of Journalism

According to *The Elements of Journalism*, a book by Bill Kovach and Tom Rosenstiel, there are nine elements of journalism. In order for a journalist to fulfill their duty of providing the people with the information they need to be free and self-governing.

Main Guidelines

1. Journalism's first obligation is to the truth.
2. Its first loyalty is to the citizens.
3. Its essence is discipline of verification.
4. Its practitioners must maintain an independence from those they cover.
5. It must serve as an independent monitor of power.
6. It must provide a forum for public criticism and compromise.
7. It must strive to make the significant interesting, and relevant.
8. It must keep the news comprehensive and proportional.
9. Its practitioners must be allowed to exercise their personal conscience.
10. Its the rights and responsibilities of citizens.

In the April 2007 edition of the book, they added the last element, *the rights and responsibilities of citizens* to make it a total of ten elements of journalism.

Professional and Ethical Standards

In the UK, all newspapers are bound by the Code of Practice of the Press Complaints Commission. This includes points like respecting people's privacy and ensuring accuracy. However, the Media Standards Trust has criticised the PCC, claiming it needs to be radically changed to secure public trust of newspapers.

This is in stark contrast to the media climate prior to the 20th Century, where the media market was dominated by smaller newspapers and pamphleteers who usually had an overt and often radical agenda, with no presumption of balance or objectivity.

Such a code of conduct can, in the real world, be

difficult to uphold consistently. Journalists who believe they are being fair or objective may give biased accounts—by reporting selectively, trusting too much to anecdote, or giving a partial explanation of actions. (See Media bias.) Even in routine reporting, bias can creep into a story through a reporter's choice of facts to summarize, or through failure to check enough sources, hear and report dissenting voices, or seek fresh perspectives.

A news organization's budget inevitably reflects decision-making about what news to cover, for what audience, and in what depth. Those decisions may reflect conscious or unconscious bias. When budgets are cut, editors may sacrifice reporters in distant news bureaus, reduce the number of staff assigned to low-income areas, or wipe entire communities from the publication's zone of interest.

Publishers, owners and other corporate executives, especially advertising sales executives, can try to use their powers over journalists to influence how news is reported and published. Journalists usually rely on top management to create and maintain a "firewall" between the news and other departments in a news organization to prevent undue influence on the news department. One journalism magazine, Columbia Journalism Review, has made it a practice to reveal examples of executives who try to influence news coverage, of executives who do not abuse their powers over journalists, and of journalists who resist such pressures.

Self-censorship is a growing problem in journalism, particularly in covering countries that sharply restrict press freedom. As commercial pressure in the media marketplace grows, media organizations are loath to lose access to high-profile countries by producing unflattering stories. For example, CNN admitted that it had practiced self-censorship in covering the Saddam Hussein regime in Iraq in order to ensure continued access after the regime had thrown out other media.

CNN correspondent Christiane Amanpour also complained of self-censorship during the invasion of Iraq due to the fear of alienating key audiences in the US. There are claims that the media are also avoiding covering stories about repression and human rights violations by the Israeli and Iranian regimes in order to maintain a presence in those countries.

Generally, publishers and consumers of journalism draw a distinction between reporting — "just the facts" — and opinion writing, often by restricting opinion columns to the editorial page and its facing or "op-ed" (opposite the editorials) page. Unsigned editorials are traditionally the official opinions of the paper's editorial board, while op-ed pages may be a mixture of syndicated columns and other contributions, frequently with some attempt to balance the voices across some political or social spectrum.

The distinction between reporting and opinion can break down. In the UK, the Press Complaints Commission states that "the Press, whilst free to be partisan, must distinguish clearly between comment, conjecture and fact" but some commentators have suggested there can sometimes be a blurring of opinion and fact. Complex stories often require summarizing and interpretation of facts, especially if there is limited time or space for a story. Stories involving great amounts of interpretation are often labelled "news analysis," but still run in a paper's news columns. The limited time for each story in a broadcast report rarely allows for such distinctions.

Legal Status

Journalists around the world often write about the

governments in their nations, and those governments have widely varying policies and practices towards journalists, which control what they can research and write, and what press organizations can publish. Many Western governments guarantee the freedom of the press, and do relatively little to restrict press rights and freedoms, while other nations severely restrict what journalists can research and/or publish.

Journalists in many nations have enjoyed some privileges not enjoyed by members of the general public, including better access to public events, crime scenes and press conferences, and to extended interviews with public officials, celebrities and others in the public eye. These privileges are available because of the perceived power of the press to turn public opinion for or against governments, their officials and policies, as well as the perception that the press often represents their consumers. These privileges extend from the legal rights of journalists but are not guaranteed by those rights.

Sometimes government officials may attempt to punish individual journalists who irk them by denying them some of these privileges extended to other journalists. Nations or jurisdictions that formally license journalists may confer special privileges and responsibilities along with those licenses, but in the United States the tradition of an independent press has avoided any imposition of government-controlled examinations or licensing. Some of the states have explicit shield laws that protect journalists from some forms of government inquiry, but those statutes' definitions of "journalist" were often based on access to printing presses and broadcast towers. A national shield law has been proposed.

Notably, in some nations, journalists are directly employed, controlled or censored by their governments. In other nations, governments who may claim to guarantee press rights actually intimidate journalists with threats of arrest, destruction or seizure of property (especially the means of production and dissemination of news content), torture or murder. Journalists who elect to cover conflicts, whether wars between nations or insurgencies within nations, often give up any expectation of protection by government, if not giving up their rights to protection by government. Journalists who are captured or detained during a conflict are expected to be treated as civilians and to be released to their national government.

Right to Protect Confidentiality of Sources

Journalists' interaction with sources sometimes involves confidentiality, an extension of freedom of the press giving journalists a legal protection to keep the identity of a source private even when demanded by police or prosecutors; withholding sources can land journalists in contempt of court, or in jail.

The scope of rights granted to journalists varies from nation to nation; in the United Kingdom, for example, the government has had more legal rights to protect what it considers sensitive information, and to force journalists to reveal the sources of leaked information, than the United States. Other nations, particularly Zimbabwe and the People's Republic of China, have a reputation of persecuting journalists, both domestic and foreign.

In the United States, there has never been a right to protect sources in a federal court. Some states provide varying degrees of such protection. However, federal courts will refuse to force journalists to reveal sources, unless the information the court seeks is highly relevant to the case, and there's no other way to get it. Journalists, like all citizens, who refuse to testify even when ordered to can be found in contempt of court and fined or jailed.

Current State

In 2008, journalism came under heavy fire. The decline of print newspapers has led to a sharp increase in job cuts for journalists. In 2008 alone, approximately 16,000 journalists were terminated – a budgetary response to declining subscription dollars and the inability to adapt to a free-news-driven society. With advertising revenues taking a harsh rapping from the transitional shift of a subscription-based/advertising model to online ad placements, the discrepancy in advertising revenue is making it difficult for traditional newspapers to survive.

The Tribune Company (owner of the *Los Angeles Times*) filed for Chapter 11 bankruptcy; The *Rocky Mountain News* (one of the country's oldest newspapers) closed its doors after 150 years of business; *The Christian Science Monitor* transitioned from its daily newspaper edition to online distribution; 120 newspapers closed their doors in the first three months of 2009; newspaper circulation was down 7% in the first six months of 2009.

Newspapers are forced to maximize their current staff in a response to declining advertising and circulation revenue. As formerly relied upon revenues shore-up, newspapers are exploring radically new ways of reaching readers. *The New York Times* has partnered with Amazon's Kindle DX to bring current subscribers and Kindle users NYT content. This, along with other social media properties, are ways in which traditional media are fighting to stay relevant in the digital age.

With the decline of print newspapers, there has been

a wave of new media journalism. New media journalism is also known as convergence journalism. Convergence journalism focuses on using social networking as a means of communication over the traditional print journalism. Many newspapers have went online because it has cut down on production costs and more people look online to find news as opposed to buying print newspapers. Recently, convergence journalism has seen an uprise in websites like Facebook and Twitter. These sites allow people to connect with each and find out anything they want to rapidly. With the evolution of new technologies, some believe the print newspaper will be wiped out completely. But for now, print and new media is still being used for journalistic purposes.

PROTECTION OF SOURCES

The protection of sources, sometimes also referred to as the confidentiality of sources or in the U.S. as the reporter's privilege, is a right accorded to journalists under the laws of many countries, as well as under international law. Simply put, it means that the authorities, including the courts, cannot compel a journalist to reveal the identity of an anonymous source for a story. The right is based on a recognition that without a strong guarantee of anonymity, many people would be deterred from coming forward and sharing information of public interests with journalists. As a result, problems such as corruption or crime might go undetected and unchallenged, to the ultimate detriment of society as a whole.

A famous instance of the use of an anonymous source is the series of articles by *Washington Post* reporters Bob Woodward and Carl Bernstein which uncovered the Watergate Scandal, ultimately leading to the resignation of US President Richard Nixon. Woodward and Bernstein relied extensively on information provided by someone known to the world only under the nickname Deep Throat. Only in 2005 did W. Mark Felt, who at the time had been Associate Director of the US Federal Bureau of Investigation, reveal that he was "Deep Throat".

Woodward and Bernstein were not forced to invoke the protection of sources, since the US authorities made no attempt to uncover the identity of "Deep Throat". An example of the legal operation of the right is the case of Bart Mos and Joost de Haas, of the Dutch daily *De Telegraaf*. In an article in January 2006, the two journalists alleged the existence of a leak in the Dutch secret services and quoted from what they claimed was an official dossier on Mink Kok, a notorious criminal. They further alleged that the dossier in question had fallen into the hands of Kok himself. A subsequent police investigation led to the prosecution of Paul H., an agent accused of selling the file in question. Upon motions by the prosecution and the defence, the investigative judge in the case ordered the disclosure of the source for the news story, on the grounds that it was necessary to safeguard national security and ensure a fair trial for H. The two journalists were subsequently detained for refusing to comply with the disclosure order, but were released on appeal after three days, on November 30. The Hague district court considered that the national security interest served by the order was minor and should not prevail over the protection of sources.

Various authorities in international law point to a recognition that a right to protection of sources is implicit in the right to freedom of expression.

In Europe, the European Court of Human Rights stated

in the 1996 case of *Goodwin v. United Kingdom* that "[p]rotection of journalistic sources is one of the basic conditions for press freedom.

Without such protection, sources may be deterred from assisting the press in informing the public on matters of public interest. As a result the vital public-watchdog role of the press may be undermined and the ability of the press to provide accurate and reliable information may be adversely affected." The Court concluded that absent an "an overriding requirement in the public interest", an order to disclose sources would violate the guarantee of free expression in Article 10 of the European Convention on Human Rights.

In the wake of *Goodwin*, the Council of Europe's Committee of Ministers issued a Recommendation to its member states on how to implement the protection of sources in their domestic legislation. The Organization for Security and Co-operation in Europe has also called on states to respect the right.

In Africa, the African Commission on Human and Peoples' Rights has adopted a *Declaration of Principles on Freedom of Expression in Africa* which includes a right to protection of sources under Principle XV.

In the Americas, protection of sources has been recognised in the *Inter-American Declaration of Principles on Freedom of Expression*, which states in Principle 8 that "every social communicator has the right to keep his/her source of information, notes, personal and professional archives confidential."

In the next chapter we will introduce you to different types of journalists, their duties, functions and other aspects.

REFERENCES

Bagdikian, Ben H. (1983). *The Media Monopoly.*

Concise History of the British Newspaper in the Eighteenth Century.

Concluding Document of the 1986 Vienna Meeting of Representatives of the Participating States of the Conference of Security and Co-operation in Euro.

Desperate Battle to Save America's Struggling Newspap.

Declaration of Principles on Freedom of Expression in A.

Herman, Edward and Noam Chomsky. 1988. *Manufacturing Consent: The Political Economy of the Mass Media.* New York: Pantheon.

http://www.pcc.org.uk/cop/practice.html; Press Complaints Commission Code of Practice.

http://www.journoworld.co.uk/Comment_in_Newspapers. html; JournoWorld - Writing Comment.

Inter-American Declaration of Principles on Freedom of Expression.

Just the Facts: How "Objectivity" Came to Define American Journalism, 1998.

Kaplan, Richard. 2002. *Politics and the American Press: The Rise of Objectivity, 1865-1920.* New York: Cambridge University Press.

Mindich, David T. Z. 1998. *Just the Facts: How "Objectivity" Came to Define American Journalism.* New York: New York University Press.

Recommendation No. R (2000)7 of the Committee of Ministers to Member States on the right of journalists not to disclose their sources of information.

Roy Greenslade - Media watchdog attacks PCC as ineffective, unaccountable and opaque; http://www.guardian.co.uk/media/greenslade/2009/feb/09/pcc-newspapers.

Schudson, Michael (1978). *Discovering the News: A social history of American newspapers.*

Schudson, Michael. 1978. *Discovering the News: A Social History of American Newspapers.* New York: Basic Books.

Schudson, Michael. 1997. "The Sociology of News Production." In *Social Meaning of News: A Text-Reader*. Dan Berkowitz, ed. Pp. 7–22. Thousand Oaks: Sage.

Silverstein, Ken, "Turkmeniscam: How Washington Lobbyists Fought to Flack for a Stalinist Dictatorship", 2008.

2

News Reporters, Analysts, Correspondents and Other Journalists

"Journalism consists in buying white paper at two cents a pound and selling it at ten cents a pound."

—*Charles A. Dana*

As we are concerned to elucidate media occupations and professionals in this book, we will introduce you new reporters, analysts, editors and others journalists in this chapter. Their duties, functions and other technical aspects are also dealt with.

NEWS REPORTER

A news reporter is a type of journalist who researches and presents information in certain types of mass media. Reporters gather their information in a variety of ways, including tips, press releases, sources (individuals with newsworthy information) and witnessing events. They perform research through interviews, public records, and other sources. The information-gathering part of the job is sometimes called "reporting" as distinct from the production part of the job, such as writing articles. Reporters generally split their time between working in a newsroom and going out to witness events or interview people. Most reporters working for major news media outlets are assigned an area to focus on, called a beat or patch. They are encouraged to cultivate sources to improve their information gathering.

Reporters working for major the Western news media usually have a university or college degree. The degree is sometimes in journalism, but in most countries, that is generally not a requirement. When hiring reporters, editors tend to give much weight to the reporter's previous work (such as newspaper clippings), even when written for a student newspaper or as part of an internship.

In the United Kingdom, editors often require that prospective trainee reporters have completed the NCTJ (National College for the Training of Journalists) preliminary exams. After 18 months to two years on the job, trainees will take a second set of exams, known collectively as the NCE. Upon completion of the NCE, the candidate is considered a fully-qualified senior reporter and usually receives a (Very Very) small pay raise. In the United States, there is no set requirement for a particular degree (and licensing journalists would be unconstitutional under the First Amendment), although almost all newspapers, wire services, television news, and radio news operations hire only college graduates and expect prior experience in journalism, either at a student publication or through an internship. Although their work can also often make them into minor celebrities, most reporters in the United States and the United Kingdom earn relatively low salaries. It is not uncommon for a reporter fresh out of college working at a small newspaper to make $20,000 annually or less. But according to the 2006 survey of journalism/mass communication graduates released in August 2007 by Dr. Lee B. Becker (University of Georgia), the average starting salary for a daily newspaper reporter in 2006 was $26,000, and the average salary at a weekly newspaper was $22,880. The average salary in radio was $23,400, while the average salary in broadcast television was $21,840, and in cable television $25,012.

Despite many college students' perceptions that newspapers pay the most poorly, both dailies and weeklies are paying more than broadcast television, which actually pays the poorest of any mass communication industry or profession (advertising graduates got $26,988 and public relations graduates got $28,964 in 2006). Around £12,000 is a typical starting wage in the UK.

In order to move to larger papers, it is common for reporters to start with newspapers in small towns and move their way up the ladder, though *The New York Times* has been known to hire reporters with only a few years experience, based on talent and expertise in particular areas.

Many reporters also start as summer interns at large papers and then move to reporting jobs at medium sized papers. The same job prospects fall into the television reporting business, with reporters starting in small markets and moving up the larger markets and to national news programmes.

Prominent Television Reporters

India

- K. Partha Sarathy (senior reporter ETV News)
- Bhargavi (reporter ETV News)
- Kamaal Khan, NDTV INDIA
- Abhishek Upadhaya, IBN7
- Raja Khan, theindiapress

Pakistan

- Hussain Mansoor
- Azam Zuhrani
- Mujahid Solnagi
- Hina Shaikh
- Wahid Jiskani
- Naz Sahito
- Muneer Deho
- Safdar Khoharo
- Aziz Ansari
- Kamran Khan
- Hamid Mir
- Asma Sherazi

United Kingdom

- Kate Adie
- Sameena Ali-Khan
- Marie Ashby
- Mark Austin
- Ian Axton
- Lisa Aziz
- Zeinab Badawi
- Llewella Bailey
- Faye Barker
- Gaynor Barnes
- Felicity Barr
- Richard Bath (presenter)
- Seán Batty

- Martin Bell
- Andrea Benfield
- John Bevir
- Sangeeta Bhabra
- Jennie Bond
- Frank Bough
- Jeremy Bowen
- Colin Brazier
- Fern Britton
- Fiona Bruce
- Lynda Bryans
- Michael Buerk
- Scott Chisholm (journalist)
- Michael Crick
- Robin Day
- Jamie Delargy
- David Dimbleby
- Jonathan Dimbleby
- Richard Dimbleby
- Steve Dixon (newsreader)
- John Doyle
- Sara Edwards
- Gavin Esler
- David Frost
- Anna Ford
- Juliette Foster
- Steve Gaisford

- Kate Garraway
- Phil Gayle
- Krishnan Guru-Murthy
- Vincent Hanna
- Brian Hanrahan
- Gordon Honeycombe
- John Humphrys
- Catherine Jacob
- Natasha Kaplinsky
- Kenneth Kendall
- Lucy Kite
- Sue Lawley
- Terry Lloyd
- Daisy McAndrew
- Trevor MacDonald
- Anne MacKenzie
- Rachel McTavish
- Paul Mason
- Cliff Michelmore
- Guy Michelmore
- Dermot Murnaghan
- Shereen Nanjiani
- Joyce Ohajah
- Rageh Omaar
- Jeremy Paxman
- Julian Pettifer
- Gaby Rado

- Sophie Raworth
- Angela Rippon
- Fyfe Robertson
- Tim Sebastian
- John Sergeant
- John Shires
- John Simpson
- Peter Sissons
- Wesley Smith
- Peter Snow
- Jon Snow
- Julia Somerville
- Owen Spencer-Thomas
- Alistair Stewart
- Hannah Stewart-Jones
- Moira Stuart
- Edward Stourton
- John Suchet
- Tamzin Sylvester
- Mark Urban
- Jeremy Vine
- Kirsty Wark
- Justin Webb
- Christine Webber
- Charles Wheeler
- Alan Wicker
- Keith Wilkinson

- Nicholas Witchell
- Alistair Yates
- Kirsty Young

United States

- National Newscasts
    - Niharika Acharya
    - Deborah Amos
    - Ed Bradley
    - Tom Brokaw
    - Chris Bury
    - Juju Chang
    - Julie Chen
    - Katie Couric
    - Anderson Cooper
    - Jason Dasey
    - John Donvan
    - Hugh Downs
    - Matt Hammer
    - Cecilia Ramirez Harris
    - Brit Hume
    - Peter Jennings
    - Ken Kashiwahara
    - Greg Kelly
    - Ted Koppel
    - Steve Kroft
    - Don Lemon
    - Jennifer Lopez

  - Javed Malik
  - Dave Marash
  - Michel Martin
  - Dan Patrick
  - John Pertzborn (journalist)
  - Mari Ramos
  - Dan Rather
  - Birmania Rios
  - Jim Roberts
  - Mark Ronchetti
  - Geraldo Rivera
  - Andy Rooney
  - Morley Safer
  - Carole Simpson
  - Leslie Stahl
  - Charlie Steiner
  - George Stephanopoulos
  - Hannah Storm
  - John Stossel
  - Boris Tenzer
  - Mike Wallace
  - Barbara Walters
  - John Yang
  - Eunice Yoon
- Local Newscasts
  - Denny Anderson
  - Priya Aujla

- Susanna Avery
- Cyndy Brucato
- Colleen Chen
- Joel Connable
- Lin Sue Cooney
- Jim Gardner
- Paola Giangiacomo
- Emily Gimmel
- Mickey Goodwin
- Julius Hunter
- Jackie Hyland
- Heather Jensen
- Beverly Kidd
- Tisha Lewis
- Nancy Loo
- Dave Malkoff
- Jackie Nespral
- Mina S Nguyen
- Vicky Nguyen
- Kent Ninomiya
- Naibe Reynoso
- Jim Roberts
- Amanda Rossetter
- Kate Sullivan
- Robbie Wright "Your Entertainment Reporter"

Israel

- Haim Yavin

Argentina

- Cristina Perez

Australia

- Richard Carleton
- George Negus
- Naomi Robson
- Abraham Gubler

Cuba

- Mirka De Arellano (on USA television, but Cuban)

Mexico

- Fernando Arau
- Ana Maria Canseco
- Maria Antonieta Collins
- Rosana Franco
- Blanca Gómez
- Joaquin Lopez Doriga
- Karla Martinez
- Raul Peimbert
- Jorge Ramos
- Maria Elena Salinas

Honduras

- Neida Sandoval

Peru

- Guillermo Descalzi

Puerto Rico

- Junior Abrams

- Maria Celeste Arraras
- Barbara Bermudo
- Rafael Bracero
- Milly Cangiano
- Nuria Cebazco
- Lourdes Collazo
- Elwood Cruz
- Enrique Cruz
- Dreuxilla Divine
- Carmen Dominicci
- Jose Esteves
- Cyd Marie Flemming
- Charito Fratichelli
- Millie Gil
- Jackie Guerrido
- Sylvia Gomez
- Anibal Gonzalez Irizarry
- Laura Hernandez
- Carmen Jovet
- Liza Lugo
- Belen Martinez Cabello
- Ada Monzon
- Carlos Ochoteco
- Cárlos Ruben Ortiz
- Evelio Otero
- John Ramos
- Luis Rigual

- Ernesto Rivera Gonzalez
- Grenda Rivera
- Jorge Rivera Nieves
- Pedro Rosa Nales
- Johanna Rosaly
- Ruben Sanchez
- Jorge Seijo
- Gloria Soltero
- Susan Soltero
- Guillermo José Torres
- Laiza Torres
- Ramon Enrique Torres
- Normando Valentin
- Luz Nereida Velez

Spain

- Leticia Ortiz (Princess of Asturias), formerly on TVE

Romania

- Nicoleta Drãgu°in - Realitatea TV, Bucharest

Russia

- Svetlana Pesotskaya

Philippines

- Cristina Canlas - Sonshine Media Network International
- Carlo Catiil - Sonshine Media Network International
- Nelson Canlas - GMA 7

- Alvin Elchico - ABS-CBN 2
- Kara David - GMA 7
- Mariz Umali - GMA 7
- Sandra Aguinaldo - GMA 7
- Jay Taruc - GMA 7
- Ralph Guzman - GMA 7
- Susan Enriquez - GMA 7
- Raffy Tima - GMA 7
- Pia Arcanghel - GMA 7
- Jun Veneracion - GMA 7
- Lei Alviz - GMA 7
- Maki Pulido - GMA 7
- Marvin Tomandao - GMA 7
- Rida Reyes - GMA 7
- Tina Panganiban-Perez - GMA 7

Trinidad & Tobago

- Giselle Mc Intyre- Ie Tv
- Melissa Williams- Ie Tv
- Rachel Thomas- Ie Tv
- Melissa Wong- Ie Tv
- Karma Ballah-Boyke
- Adonis Ballah
- Odessa Kerr
- Sharon Hamilton - The TV6 News
- Robert Demas
- Colleen Holder
- Alicia Lawrence

- Satesh Mahabir
- Sandra Maharaj - C News
- Sasha Mohammed - The TV6 News
- Sampson Nanton
- Karen Cozier Phillip - The TV6 News
- Stacy-Ann Providence
- Hema Ramkissoon - C News
- Yolande Thomas
- Rosemarie Sant
- Jesse-May Ventour
- Ashford Jackman - TV6 Sports
- Charlene Stuart - The TV6 News
- Fabien Pierre - The TV6 News
- Sharmilla Persad - The TV6 News
- Marcia Hope - The TV6 News
- Nicola Lashley - The TV6 News
- Joel Villafana - TV6 Sports
- Shabaka Kambon - The TV6 News
- James Saunders - TV6 Sports
- Nathalie Chrysosthom - The TV6 News

Turkey

- Fatih Altaylý
- Fulin Arýkan
- Deniz Arman
- Tûba Atav
- Jülide Ate°
- Mehmet Barlas

- Mithat Bereket
- Mehmet Ali Birand
- Murat Birsel
- Emre Buga
- Mirgün Cabas
- Hakan Çelik
- Sevinç Satýroðlu
- Murat Çelik
- Pelin Çift
- Sonay Dikkaya
- Uður Dündar
- Erhan Ertürk
- Gülgûn Feyman
- Jülide Gülizar
- Banu Güven
- Korcan Karar
- Ali Kýrca
- Zafer Kiraz
- Reha Muhtar
- Murat Ongun
- Cem Öðretir
- Ece Özbek
- Nazlý Öztarhan
- Þirin Payzýn
- Defne Samyeli
- Defne Sarýsoy
- Esra Sert

- ªebnem Sunar Küçük
- Nazlý Tolga
- Nermin Tuðuþlu
- Saba Tümer
- Ece Üner
- Türkan Varol
- Kaan Yakuphan
- Arzu Zengin
- Gürkan Zengin
- Orkun Yazgan

Uruguay

- Pedro Sevcec

JOURNALIST

Basically, journalist is a person who practices journalism, the gathering and dissemination of information about current events, trends, issues, and people while striving for viewpoint that is not biased. Reporters are one type of journalist. They create reports as a profession for broadcast or publication in mass media such as newspapers, television, radio, magazines, documentary film, and the Internet.

Reporters find sources for their work, their reports can be either spoken or written, and they are often expected to report in the most objective and unbiased way to serve the public good. A columnist is a journalist who writes pieces that appear regularly in newspapers or magazines. Depending on the context, the term *journalist* also includes various types of editors and visual journalists, such as photographers, graphic artists, and page designers. Journalists put the information in their own words, making it creative in their own way so it will catch the reader's or viewer's attention.

Modern media, including the creation of Internet-based news sources and the possibility that citizen journalism will greatly expand the field, has made it all but impossible to identify which journalists are notable, in the sense that they could be identified in the past. The global justice protests in Seattle (1999) gave rise to the independent media movement, exemplified by, among others, the Indymedia network, a collective of independent media organizations and hundreds of journalists offering grassroots, non-corporate coverage.

Kid Journalists

The Scholastic News Kids Press Corps is a group of kids aged 8 -14 who report events from across the United States for Scholastic News website and classroom magazines.

Some journalists in the United States adhere to the standards and norms expressed in the Society of Professional Journalists ethical code. Foremost in the minds of most practicing journalists is the issue of maintaining credibility, "Professional integrity is the cornerstone of a journalist's credibility."

Journalists' Education and Training

Journalists often either receive training directly in the type of news field that they wish to enter, or through various institutions of higher education.

Australia

In Australia, the most notable alumni of journalists come from Charles Sturt University, Jschool, RMIT University and University of Technology, Sydney.

United States

From Columbia University and Point Park University's School of Communications and Journalism on the East Coast of America, to University of Southern California and Arizona State University's Walter Cronkite School of Journalism and Mass Communication on the West Coast, there is a broad range of options for beginning journalists to choose from when entering the field.

INTERN

An intern is one who works in a temporary position with an emphasis on on-the-job training rather than merely employment, making it similar to an apprenticeship. Interns are usually college or university students, but they can also be high school students or post graduate adults seeking skills for a new career. Student internships provide opportunities for students to gain experience in their field, determine if they have an interest in a particular career, create a network of contacts, or gain school credit. Internships provide the employers with cheap or free labor for (typically) low-level tasks (stereotypically including fetching coffee for the office), and also the prospect of interns returning to the company after completing their education and requiring little or no training. An internship may be either paid, unpaid or partially paid (in the form of a stipend). Paid internships are most common in the medical, architecture science, engineering, law, business (especially accounting and finance), technology and advertising fields. Internships in non-profit organization such as charities and think tanks are often unpaid, volunteer positions.

Internships may be part-time or full-time; typically they are part-time during the university year and full-time in the summer, and they typically last 6-12 weeks, but can be shorter or longer. The act of job shadowing may also constitute as interning.

Internship positions are available from businesses, government departments, non-profit groups and organizations. Due to strict labor laws, European internships, though mostly unpaid, are popular among non-Europeans to gain international exposure on one's resume and for foreign language improvement.

Types of Internships

An intern type means doing internship in an organization or in specific subject of study. Internships exist in various industries and settings. Here are two primary types of internships that exist in the United States.

1. *Work experience internship:* Most often this will be in the second or third year of the school period. The placement can be from 2 months to sometimes even one full school year. During this period the student is supposed to use the things he/she has learned in school and put it in practice. This way the student gets work experience in their field of study. The gained experience will be helpful to finish up the last year of the study.

2. *Research internship (graduation) or dissertation internship:* This is mostly done by students that are in their last year. With this kind of internship a student does research for a particular company. The company can have something that they feel like they need to improve, or the student can choose a topic within the company themselves. The results of the research study will be put in a report and often will have to be presented.

Paying for an Internship

Some companies will find and place students in

internships for a fee; such internships are mostly unpaid. In some cases companies charge to assist with a search, promising to refund their fees if no internship is found. What is included in such paid programmes varies by company.

Overall, the advantages are that they provide internship placements at reputable companies, provide controlled housing in a new city, mentorship and support throughout the summer, networking, weekend activities in some programmes, and sometimes academic credit. Another form of paying for internships is through charity auctions, where a company with an internship will select a charity to get the proceeds of the auction.

In some cases, companies have created internships simply to help charities. Fee-based programmes, and charity auctions, restrict internship opportunities to students in wealthier families who can afford paying thousands of dollars while the student works for little or no wages, in exchange for improving professional work opportunities after graduation. But the head of one company specializing in such internships said that "The average student comes from the middle class, and their parents dig deep" to pay for it. He said that his company had begun, in 2008, to fund scholarships and grants for low-income applicants.

International Student Internships

Many students do internships in a different country to get international experience and learn an extra language. The meaning of an internship can be different around the globe.

Spain

At Spanish universities it is uncommon to do an internship during the education period. The real working experiment for them starts when they are done with their study. However, Spanish companies are getting more used to having students doing an internship at their company nowadays. Mostly these are international students from other European countries. Spain is a popular country for students to go to for a short period of time to do an internship. A lot of times students want to learn Spanish, and this is a perfect opportunity for them to do so. Another reason to go to Spain for an internship could be the opportunity to increase their cultural awareness or to experience working in an international setting.

Students found that it is hard to get in contact with most Spanish Businesses. The best way to find a good company to work at will be with the help of a placement organization. The normal stage compensation rate in Spain is around €800.

Denmark

It is not seen as appropriate to work without pay unless it is done as part of a work-trial where a person is tested by the authorities as part of plan to get the individual back into the workspace. The company is then compensated and the intern gets welfare during this period, which normally lasts about three months. The Trade Unions monitor this area very thoroughly so an intern cannot result in the loss of a paid job. A new system of qualification for higher education imposed by the Department of Education does punish those students who take a period off to work for charity.

Italy

Internships (commonly referred to with the french term "stage") are being used by companies more often. Usually, students have to participate in at least one when still at university, but also after graduating. It is common, especially among Italians, but also among foreign students. Usually internships in Italy are not paid. This is a real problem for young graduates, since companies often take stagiare just to save money, not guaranteeing a position after the work experience has finished. Sometimes there isn't a real effort to train them.

UK, Canada and Australia

Internships are often referred to as 'sandwich placements' in the UK and are validated work experienced opportunity as part of a degree programme. University staff give students access to vacancies and students apply direct to employers.

Some universities hold fairs and exhibitions to encourage students to consider the option and to enable students to meet potential employers. In the modern labor market graduates with work experience in the form of sandwich placements are not only deemed more desirable to employers but also research has demonstrated they attain higher level degree classifications than those graduates without such experience. In these countries they have split the types of internship in unpaid or paid. The unpaid internship are mostly the ones that are chosen by students who are either still in school and doing an internship as part of the requirements of school or who have just left school. The purpose of these internships are to get understanding about how work is conducted in the English-speaking world and to improve one's English. Another plus is to learn about work ethic and to experience cultural diversity. The paid internship is mostly for people that want to come to these countries to improve their English. The job for them is not something that they are specialized in, but see it as something that will give them enough money to support their living in these countries.

France

At the French universities it is also most common to do an internship, in France called stage, during the third or fourth year of your studies. The duration of the internships varies from 2 to 6 months, but very seldom longer than that. In France it is also becoming more popular to do an internship after one has finished studying. Mostly for students that did not get the chance to do an internship during their study career, and try to gain some working experience this way. Most times with the thought of getting hired after the internship period. An internship in France is also popular for international students. The number one reason to do an internship in France is to learn the language. A lot of French companies seem to be open to students from different countries. It is a big plus for companies to have employees who speak multiple languages.

Netherlands

In the Netherlands it is also common to do an internship during college. Just like in France it is called stage. Students will go intern for approximately 5 months. Companies are not obligated to pay the student, so sometimes small companies won't pay anything. The normal stage compensation rate in Holland is around €800.

Germany

In Germany there are different kinds of internships as well. As in most other countries, most students take their internship during the third or fourth year of their degree. One of the biggest differences to other countries is that most internships are paid. The average pay is €900 a month because jobs under €900 are free of social contributions. In some fields of study it is common to write the final thesis in a company. Another type of internship has emerged, the post graduation internship. The high unemployment in Germany during the last years has made it hard for people to find the right job, especially for people that have just graduated and lack work experience. Because of this, many offer to do an internship at their preferred place of employment while earning very little, in the hope of landing a job there in the future.

PUNDIT (EXPERT)

A pundit is someone who offers to mass-media their opinion or commentary on a particular subject area (most typically political analysis, the social sciences or sport) on which they are presumed to be knowledgeable. The term has been increasingly applied to popular media personalities. In certain cases, it may be used in a derogatory manner as well.

The term originates from the Sanskrit term, meaning learned. It refers to someone who is erudite in various subjects and who conducts religious ceremonies and offers counsel to the king or mayor.

From at least the early 19th century, a Pundit of the Supreme Court in Colonial India was an officer of the judiciary who advised British judges on questions of Hindu law. In Anglo-Indian use, *pundit* also referred to a native of India who was trained and employed by the British to survey inaccessible regions beyond the British frontier.

Speculation exists that the term's contemporary use may have its origins in a Yale University society known as "The Pundits" which, founded in 1884, developed a reputation for including among its members the school's most incisive and humorous critics of contemporary society. The group's late-nineteenth and early-twentieth century focus on lampooning the social and political world were well-documented in the university's yearbook and the Yale Daily News, the entries of which are considered among the first use of the term "Pundit" to refer to a critic of or expert on contemporary matters.

Several members of the society have also gone on to become leading political pundits, including Pulitzer Prize-winning author and energy expert Daniel Yergin. Other notable Yale Pundits include A. Whitney Griswold, Lewis H. Lapham and Joe Lieberman. In the English-speaking West, *pundits* write signed articles in print media (blurbs included), and appear on radio, television, or the internet with opinions on current events. Television pundits may also be referred to as *talking heads*. Punditry has become a more popular vehicle in nightly newscasts on American cable news networks. A rise of partisanship among popular pundits began with Bill O'Reilly of Fox News Channel. His opinion-oriented format led him to ratings success and has led others, including Lou Dobbs, Keith Olbermann, and Nancy Grace, to express their opinions on matters on their own respective programmes.

Internet authors trying to create a name for themselves by non-traditional means, may refer to themselves as pundits, and in fact can be considered experts of their particular life experiences or observations.

In sports commentating, a "pundit" or color commentator may be partnered with a play-by-play announcer who will describe the action while asking the pundit for analysis. Alternatively, pundits may be asked for their opinions during breaks in the play.

COLUMNIST

A columnist is a journalist who writes for publication in a

series, creating copy that can sometimes be strongly opinionated. Columns appear in newspapers, magazines and other publications, including blogs on the Internet. Readers often open a publication with an expectation of reading a new essay by a specific writer who offers a personal point of view. Some columnists appear on a daily basis and later reprint the same material in book collections. In defining a column, Dictionary.com provides a breakdown of a few popular subjects covered by columnists: "A regular feature or series of articles in a newspaper, magazine, or the like, usually having a readily identifiable heading and the byline of the writer or editor, that reports or comments upon a particular field of interest, as politics, theater, or etiquette, or which may contain letters from readers, answers to readers' queries, etc." In at least one situation, a column expanded to become an entire successful magazine. When Cyrus Curtis founded the *Tribune and Farmer* in 1879, it was a four-page weekly with an annual subscription rate of 50 cents. He introduced a women's column by his wife, Louise Knapp Curtis, and it proved so popular that in 1883, he decided to publish it as a separate monthly supplement, *Ladies Journal and Practical Housekeeper*, edited by Louise Curtis. With 25,000 subscribers by the end of its first year, it was such a success that Curtis sold *Tribune and Farmer* to put his energy into the new publication, which became the *Ladies Home Journal*.

Radio and Television

Newspaper columnists of the 1930s and 1940s, such as Franklin Pierce Adams (aka FPA), Nick Kenny, Jimmie Fidler, Walter Winchell. Louella Parsons, Drew Pearson, Ed Sullivan and Walter Winchell, achieved a celebrity status and used their syndicated columns as a springboard to move into radio and television. In some cases, such as

Winchell and Parsons, their radio programmes were quite similar in format to their newspaper columns. Rona Barrett began as a Hollywood gossip columnist in 1957, duplicating her print tactics on television by the mid-1960s. One of the more famous syndicated columnists of the 1920s and 1930s, O. O. McIntyre, declined offers to do a radio series because he felt it would interfere and diminish the quality of writing in his column, "New York Day by Day."

Books

However, FPA and McIntyre both collected their columns into a series of books, as did other columnists. McIntyre's book, *The Big Town: New York Day by Day* (1935) was a bestseller. FPA's *The Melancholy Lute* (1936), collected selections from three decades of his columns. H. Allen Smith's first humor book, *Low Man on a Totem Pole* (1941) and his two following books were so popular during World War II that they kept Smith on the *New York Herald Tribune*'s Best Seller List for 100 weeks and prompted a collection of all three in *3 Smiths in the Wind* (1946).

While Smith's column, *The Totem Pole*, was syndicated by United Features, he told Time: Just between you and me it's tough. A typewriter can be a pretty formidable contraption when you sit down in front of it and say: 'All right, now I'm going to be funny.' *The Miami Herald* promotes humor columnist Dave Barry with this description: "Dave Barry has been at *The Miami Herald* since 1983.

A Pulitzer Prize winner for commentary, he writes about issues ranging from the international economy to exploding toilets." Barry has collected his columns into a series of successful books, and the newspaper offers a selection of memorable Barry columns on its website.

Types of Columnists

- agony aunt, an advice columnist
- critic reviewer
- editorial opinion columnist
- gossip columnist
- humor columnist
- food columnist

PHOTOGRAPHER

In conventional terms, a photographer is a person who takes a photograph using a camera. A *professional photographer* uses photography to make a living whilst an amateur photographer does not earn a living and typically takes photographs for pleasure and to record an event, place or person for future enjoyment.

Photographers are often categorized based on the subjects they photograph. Some photographers explore subjects typical of paintings such as landscape, still life, and portraiture.

Notably, photographers specialize in subjects unique to photography, including street photography, documentary photography, fashion photography, wedding photography, war photography, photojournalism and commercial photography. Paparazzi are photographers who take candid photographs and, quite commonly, pre-arranged photographs made to appear candid, of celebrities.

NEWS ANALYSTS, REPORTERS, AND CORRESPONDENTS

Competition will be keen for jobs at large metropolitan and national newspapers, broadcast stations, and magazines; small publications and broadcast stations and online newspapers and magazines should provide the best opportunities. Most employers prefer individuals with a bachelor's degree in journalism or mass communications and experience gained at school newspapers or broadcasting stations or through internships with news organizations. Jobs often involve long, irregular hours and pressure to meet deadlines.

Nature of the Work

News analysts, reporters, and correspondents gather information, prepare stories, and make broadcasts that inform us about local, State, national, and international events; present points of view on current issues; and report on the actions of public officials, corporate executives, interest groups, and others who exercise power. News analysts—also called newscasters or news anchors—examine, interpret, and broadcast news received from various sources.

News anchors present news stories and introduce videotaped news or live transmissions from on-the-scene reporters. News correspondents report on news occurring in the large U.S. and foreign cities where they are stationed. In covering a story, reporters investigate leads and news tips, look at documents, observe events at the scene, and interview people. Reporters take notes and also may take photographs or shoot videos. At their office, they organize the material, determine the focus or emphasis, write their stories, and edit accompanying video material. Many reporters enter information or write stories using laptop computers and electronically submit the material to their offices from remote locations.

In some cases, newswriters write a story from information collected and submitted by reporters. Radio and television reporters often compose stories and report "live" from the scene. At times, they later tape an introduction to or commentary on their story in the studio. Some journalists also interpret the news or offer opinions to readers, viewers, or listeners. In this role, they are called commentators or columnists. Newscasters at large stations and networks usually specialize in a particular type of news, such as sports or weather.

Weathercasters, also called weather reporters, report current and forecasted weather conditions. They gather information from national satellite weather services, wire services, and local and regional weather bureaus. Some weathercasters are trained meteorologists and can develop their own weather forecasts. Sportscasters select, write, and deliver sports news. This may include interviews with sports personalities and coverage of games and other sporting events. General-assignment reporters write about newsworthy occurrences—such as accidents, political rallies, visits of celebrities, or business closings—as assigned. Large newspapers and radio and television stations assign reporters to gather news about specific topics, such as crime or education. Some reporters specialize in fields such as health, politics, foreign affairs, sports, theater, consumer affairs, social events, science, business, or religion. Investigative reporters cover stories that may take many days or weeks of information gathering.

Some publications use teams of reporters instead of assigning each reporter one specific topic, allowing reporters to cover a greater variety of stories. News teams may include reporters, editors, graphic artists, and photographers working together to complete a story. Reporters on small publications cover all aspects of the news. They take photographs, write headlines, lay out pages, edit wire-service stories, and write editorials.

Some also solicit advertisements, sell subscriptions, and perform general office work. The work of news analysts, reporters, and correspondents is usually hectic. They are under great pressure to meet deadlines. Broadcasts sometimes are aired with little or no time for preparation. Some news analysts, reporters, and correspondents work in comfortable, private offices; others work in large rooms filled with the sound of keyboards and computer printers, as well as the voices of other reporters. Curious onlookers, police, or other emergency workers can distract those reporting from the scene for radio and television. Covering wars, political uprisings, fires, floods, and similar events is often dangerous. Reporters on morning papers often work from late afternoon until midnight. Radio and television reporters usually are assigned to a day or evening shift.

Magazine reporters usually work during the day. Reporters sometimes have to change their work hours to meet a deadline or to follow late-breaking developments. Their work demands long hours, irregular schedules, and some travel. Because many stations and networks are on the air 24 hours a day, newscasters can expect to work unusual hours.

Training and Other Qualifications

Most employers prefer individuals with a bachelor's degree in journalism or mass communications, but some hire graduates with other majors. They look for experience at school newspapers or broadcasting stations, and internships with news organizations. Large-city newspapers and stations also may prefer candidates with a degree in a subject-matter specialty such as economics, political science, or business. Some large newspapers and broadcasters may hire only experienced reporters.

Education and training. More than 1,500 institutions offer programmes in communications, journalism, and related programmes. In 2007, 109 of these were accredited by the Accrediting Council on Education in Journalism and Mass Communications. Most of the courses in a typical curriculum are in liberal arts; the remaining courses are in journalism. Examples of journalism courses are introductory mass media, basic reporting and copy editing, history of journalism, and press law and ethics. Students planning a career in broadcasting take courses in radio and television news and production. Those planning newspaper or magazine careers usually specialize in news-editorial journalism. To create stories for online media, they need to learn to use computer software to combine online story text with audio and video elements and graphics. Some schools also offer a master's or Ph.D. degree in journalism. Some graduate programmes are intended primarily as preparation for news careers, while others prepare journalism teachers, researchers and theorists, and advertising and public relations workers.

A graduate degree may help those looking to advance more quickly. High school courses in English, journalism, and social studies provide a good foundation for college programmes. Useful college liberal arts courses include English with an emphasis on writing, sociology, political science, economics, history, and psychology. Courses in computer science, business, and speech are useful as well. Fluency in a foreign language is necessary in some jobs. Employers report that practical experience is the most important part of education and training.

Upon graduation many students already have gained much practical experience through part-time or summer jobs or through internships with news organizations. Most newspapers, magazines, and broadcast news organizations offer reporting and editing internships. Work on high school and college newspapers, at broadcasting stations, or on community papers or U.S. Armed Forces publications also provides practical training. In addition, journalism scholarships, fellowships, and assistantships awarded to college journalism students by universities, newspapers, foundations, and professional organizations are helpful. Experience as a stringer or freelancer—a part-time reporter who is paid only for stories printed—is advantageous.

Other qualifications. Reporters typically need more than good word-processing skills. Computer graphics and desktop-publishing skills also are useful. Computer-assisted reporting involves the use of computers to analyze data in search of a story. This technique and the interpretation of the results require computer skills and familiarity with databases.

Knowledge of news photography also is valuable for entry-level positions, which sometimes combine the responsibilities of a reporter with those of a camera operator or photographer. Reporters should be dedicated to providing accurate and impartial news. Accuracy is important, both to serve the public and because untrue or libelous statements can lead to lawsuits. A nose for news, persistence, initiative, poise, resourcefulness, a good memory, and physical stamina are important, as is the emotional stability to deal with pressing deadlines, irregular hours, and dangerous assignments.

Broadcast reporters and news analysts must be comfortable on camera. All reporters must be at ease in unfamiliar places and with a variety of people. Positions involving on-air work require a pleasant voice and appearance.

Most reporters start at small publications or broadcast stations as general assignment reporters or copy editors. They are usually assigned to cover court proceedings and civic and club meetings, summarize speeches, and write obituaries. With experience, they report more difficult assignments or specialize in a particular field. Large publications and stations hire few recent graduates; as a rule, they require new reporters to have several years of experience. Some news analysts and reporters can advance by moving to larger newspapers or stations. A few experienced reporters become columnists, correspondents, writers, announcers, or public relations specialists. Others become editors in print journalism or programme managers in broadcast journalism, who supervise reporters. Some eventually become broadcasting or publishing industry managers.

Employment & Job Outlook

News analysts, reporters, and correspondents held about 67,000 jobs in 2006. About 59 percent worked for newspaper, periodical, book, and directory publishers. Another 23 percent worked in radio and television broadcasting. About 11 percent of news analysts, reporters, and correspondents were self-employed (freelancers or stringers).

There is expected to be little or no change in employment through 2016. Competition will continue to be keen for jobs on large metropolitan and national newspapers, broadcast stations and networks, and magazines. Small broadcast stations and publications and online newspapers and magazines should provide the best opportunities. Talented writers who can handle highly specialized scientific or technical subjects will have an advantage.

Employment of news analysts, reporters, and

correspondents is expected to grow 2 percent between 2006 and 2016, which is considered to be little or no change in employment. Many factors will contribute to the limited job growth in this occupation. Consolidation and convergence should continue in the publishing and broadcasting industries. As a result, companies will be better able to allocate their news analysts, reporters, and correspondents to cover news stories. Constantly improving technology also is allowing workers to do their jobs more efficiently, another factor that will limit the number of workers needed to cover a story or certain type of news.

However, the continued demand for news will create some job opportunities. Job openings also will result from the need to replace workers who leave their occupations permanently; some news analysts, reporters, and correspondents find the work too stressful and hectic or do not like the lifestyle, and transfer to other occupations.

Competition will continue to be keen for jobs on large metropolitan and national newspapers, broadcast stations and networks, and magazines. Job opportunities will be best for applicants in the expanding world of new media, such as online newspapers or magazines. Small, local papers and news stations also will provide greater job prospects for potential reporters and news analysts.

For beginning newspaper reporters, freelancing will supply more opportunities for employment as well. Students with a background in journalism as well as another specific subject matter, such as politics, economics, or biology, will have an advantage over those without additional background knowledge. Journalism graduates have the background for work in closely related fields such as advertising and public relations, and many take jobs in these fields. Other graduates accept sales, managerial, or other nonmedia positions. The number of job openings in the newspaper and broadcasting industries—in which news analysts, reporters, and correspondents are employed—is sensitive to economic upswings and downturns because these industries depend on advertising revenue.

Remuneration

Salaries for news analysts, reporters, and correspondents vary widely. Median annual earnings of reporters and correspondents were $33,470 in May 2006. The middle 50 percent earned between $24,370 and $51,700. The lowest 10 percent earned less than $19,180, and the highest 10 percent earned more than $73,880. Median annual earnings of reporters and correspondents were $31,690 in newspaper, periodical, book, and directory publishing, and $38,050 in radio and television broadcasting. Median annual earnings of broadcast news analysts were $46,710 in May 2006. The middle 50 percent earned between $30,080 and $83,370. The lowest 10 percent earned less than $22,430, and the highest 10 percent earned more than $145,600. Median annual earnings of broadcast news analysts were $48,790 in radio and television broadcasting.

EDITING

Editing is the process of preparing language, images, sound, video, or film through correction, condensation, organization, and other modifications in various media. A person who edits is called an editor. In a sense, the editing process originates with the idea for the work itself and continues in the relationship between the author and the editor. Editing is, therefore, also a practice that includes creative skills, human relations, and a precise set of methods.

Print Media

There are various levels of editorial positions in publishing. Typically, one finds junior editorial assistants reporting to the senior-level editorial staff and directors who report to senior executive editors. Senior executive editors are responsible for developing a product to its final release. The smaller the publication, the more these roles run together.

In particular, the substantive editor and copy editor often overlap: fact-checking and rewriting can be the responsibility of either. Newspaper and wire services copy editors correct spelling, grammar, and matters of house style, design pages and select of news stories for inclusion. At UK and Australian newspapers, the term is "sub-editor." They may choose the layout of the publication and communicate with the printer — a *production editor*. This and similar jobs are also called "layout editor," "design editor," "news designer," or — more so in the past — "makeup editor." Magazine editors include a top-level editor may be called an *editor-in-chief*. Frequent and esteemed contributors to a magazine may acquire a title of *editor at-large* or *contributing editor*.) In the book publishing industry, editors organize anthologies and other compilations, produce definitive editions of a classic author's works ("scholarly editor"); and organize and manage contributions to a multi-author book (symposium editor or volume editor). Finding marketable ideas and presenting them to appropriate authors: a *sponsoring editor*. Obtaining copy or recruiting authors such as: an *acquisitions editor* or a *commissioning editor* for a publishing house. Improving an author's writing so that they indeed say what they mean to say in an effective manner; a *substantive editor*.

Depending on the writer's competence, this editing can sometimes turn into ghost writing. Substantive editing is seldom a title. Many types of editors do this type of work, either in-house at a publisher or on an independent basis. Changes to the publishing industry since the 1980s have resulted in nearly all copy editing of book manuscripts being outsourced to freelance copy editors.

EXECUTIVE EDITOR

The top editor sometimes has the title executive editor or editor-in-chief. This person is generally responsible for the content of the publication. The exception is that newspapers that are large enough usually have a separate editor for the editorials and opinion pages in order to have a complete separation of its news reporting and its editorial content.

The executive editor sets the publication standards for performance, as well as for motivating and developing the staff. The executive editor is also responsible for developing and maintaining the publication budget. In concert with the publisher and the operating committee, the executive editor is responsible for strategic and operational planning.

Newspapers

Editors at newspapers supervise journalists and improve their work. Newspaper editing encompasses a variety of titles and functions. These include:

- Copy editors
- Department editors
- Managing editors and assistant or deputy managing editors (the managing editor is often second in line after the top editor)

- News editors, who oversee the news desks
- Photo or picture editors
- Section editors and their assistants, such as for business, features, and sports
- Editorial Page Editor who oversees the coverage on the editorial page. This includes chairing the Editorial Board and assigning editorial writing responsibilities. The editorial page editor may also oversee the op-ed page or those duties are assigned to a separate op-ed editor.
- Top editors, who may be called *editor in chief, executive editor* or sometimes just *editor*
- Readers' editors, sometimes known as the ombudsman, who arbitrate complaints
- Wire editors, who choose and edit articles from various international wire services, and are usually part of the copy desk
- Administrative editors (who actually don't edit but perform duties such as recruiting and directing training)

The term *city editor* is used differently in North America and South America, where it refers to the editor responsible for the news coverage of a newspaper's local circulation area (also sometimes called *metro editor*), than in the United Kingdom, where it refers to the editor responsible for coverage of business in the City of London and, by extension, coverage of business and finance in general.

Scholarly Books and Journals

Editors of scholarly books and journals are of three types, each with particular responsibilities: the *acquisitions* *editor* (or *commissioning editor* in Britain), who contracts with the author to produce the copy, the *project editor* or *production editor,* who sees the copy through its stages from manuscript through bound book and usually assumes most of the budget and schedule responsibilities, and the *copy editor* or *manuscript editor,* who performs the tasks of readying the copy for conversion into printed form. The primary difference between copy editing scholarly books and journals and other sorts of copy editing lies in applying the standards of the publisher to the copy. Most scholarly publishers have a preferred style guide, usually a combination of Merriam-Webster's Collegiate Dictionary and either the *Chicago Manual of Style*, the *MLA Style Manual*, or the *APA Publication Manual* in the US or New Hart's Rules in the UK.

Since scholars often have strong preferences, very often a publisher will adopt different styles for different fields. For instance, psychologists prefer the APA style, while linguists might prefer the MLA style. These guidelines offer sound advice on making cited sources complete and correct and making the presentation scholarly.

Technical Editing

Technical editing involves reviewing text written on a technical topic, and identifying errors related to the use of language in general or adherence to a specific style guide. This activity ensures that documentation is of good quality.

In large companies, experienced writers are dedicated to the technical editing function; in organizations that cannot afford dedicated editors, experienced writers typically peer-edit text produced by their relatively less experienced colleagues. It helps if the technical editor is familiar with the subject being edited, but that is not always essential.

The "technical" knowledge that an editor gains over time while working on a particular product or technology does give the editor an edge over another who has just started editing content related to that product or technology. In the long run, however, the skills that really matter are attention to detail, the ability to sustain focus while working through lengthy pieces of text on complex topics, tact in dealing with writers, and excellent communication skills. Revising is also another form of editing.

3

Types of Journalism

> "We ought never to fasten our ships to one small anchor, nor our life to a single hope."
>
> —*Epictetus*

Every aspirant for opting career in the field of mass media and journalism must have a thorough acquaintance with various types of journalism. No doubt, the various types of journalism have overlapping functions, but it is necessary to have an accurate understanding of each of them.

Here in the present chapter we will introduce you to different types of journalism with their unique nature and other specifications which will help you apt for a specific field as per your aptitude.

NEW JOURNALISM

New Journalism was a style of 1960s and 1970s news writing and journalism which used literary techniques deemed unconventional at the time. The term was codified with its current meaning by Tom Wolfe in a 1973 collection of journalism articles he published as *The New Journalism*, which included works by himself, Truman Capote, Hunter S. Thompson, Norman Mailer, Joan Didion, Robert Christgau, and others.

Articles in the New Journalism style tended not to be found in newspapers, but rather in magazines such as *The New Yorker*, *New York Magazine*, *The Atlantic Monthly*, *Rolling Stone*, *Esquire Magazine*, *CoEvolution Quarterly*, and for a short while in the early 1970s, *Scanlan's Monthly*.

Major Characteristics

Remarkably, Wolfe identified the four main devices New Journalists borrowed from literary fiction:

- Dialogue in full (Conversational speech rather than quotations and statements)
- Telling the story using scenes rather than historical narrative as much as possible
- Recording everyday details such as behaviour, possessions, friends and family (which indicate the "status life" of the character)
- Third-person point-of-view (present every scene through the eyes of a particular character)

In fact, of these elements, New Journalism is not fiction. It maintains elements of reporting including strict adherence to factual accuracy and the writer being the primary source. To get "inside the head" of a character, the journalist asks the subject what they were thinking or how they felt.

Wolfe unwittingly published his first New Journalism-style article in 1963 after having trouble writing an assignment about hot rod culture and sending his editor a letter containing his thoughts on the article. The editor chose simply to remove the salutation from Wolfe's letter and print it as received.

Journalists recognised as using the style include Norman Mailer, Joan Didion, Darrell Bob Houston, Truman Capote,

P. J. O'Rourke, George Plimpton, Terry Southern, Richard Ben Cramer and Gay Talese. Hunter S. Thompson was a major practitioner of new journalism and gonzo journalism, his own particular style. Thompson's first book, *Hell's Angels: The Strange and Terrible Saga of the Outlaw Motorcycle Gangs*, is a more conventional piece, and shows the beginnings of a more memoir-based approach to reportage. Gay Talese's 1966 article for Esquire, *Frank Sinatra Has a Cold*, was an influential piece of new journalism that gave a detailed portrait of Frank Sinatra without ever interviewing him.

New journalism writers brought new approaches to areas already covered by the mainstream press. The psychedelic movement was something that many of the writers of the period covered, such as in Tom Wolfe's *The Electric Kool-Aid Acid Test.* The Vietnam War was another common topic, as was the political turmoil on the homefront. Terry Southern's Grooving in Chi documented the 1968 Chicago National Democratic Convention for Esquire Magazine in new journalism manner. New journalism's techniques were also applied to less obvious subjects, such as financial markets.

Some authors of conventional fiction switched to writing in the style of new journalism, such as Truman Capote's *In Cold Blood*, and Norman Mailer's *Armies of the Night*. However, neither author ever agreed to their style's comparison to Wolfe's school of narration, nor did many others who have been retrospectively promoted as being members and therein associated. Much to the contrary, many of these writers would deny that their work was generically relevant to other new journalists at the time. This may be because, during such a politically torn period, these authors were politically across the spectrum, from the New Left to the Old Right.

NARRATIVE JOURNALISM

Narrative journalism is commonly referred to as literary journalism, which is defined as creative nonfiction that, if well written, contains accurate and well-researched information and also holds the interest of the reader. It is also related to immersion journalism, a term used to describe a situation when a writer follows a subject or theme for a long period of time (weeks or months) and details an individual's experiences from a deeply personal perspective. Narrative journalism is the interpretation of a story and the way in which the journalist portrays it, be it fictional or non-fictional. In easier words, it tells a story.

It is significant to note that Truman Capote's *In Cold Blood* is a historic example of narrative journalism in novel form. Published in 1965, the book was the first "nonfiction novel" and helped show journalists the possibility of using creative writing techniques while holding to the guidelines of journalism. Though Capote claims to have invented this new form of journalism, the origin of a movement of creative writing in journalism is often thought to have occurred much earlier.

Characteristics of narrative journalism can be found in Daniel Defoe's writing in the 1700s, as well as in writings of Mark Twain in the 19th century and James Agee, Ernest Hemingway and John Steinbeck in the World War II period. Furthers Tom Wolfe also wrote *The New Journalism* in 1974 and is credited for popularizing discussion on the appropriateness of narrative in journalism. He cites Gay Talese with being the "father" of new journalism, and exemplifies the foundations of narrative journalism in his compilation "The Gay Talese Reader".

Now, many nonfiction novels use narrative journalism to tell their stories. Print publications such as *Harper's*, *The New Yorker*, *Esquire*, *Rolling Stone*, and *The Village Voice* are also welcome homes to narrative journalists.

Mainstream newspaper publications are still wary of supporting narrative journalism too much due to time and space constraints, and will often print the occasional narrative in a Sunday features or supplemental magazine. The definitions of narrative journalism are many and varied. Some prefer to refer to literary journalism, or creative non-fiction. Simply put, narrative is the way in which a story is constructed through a particular point of view and arrangement of events.

The Nieman Programme on Narrative Journalism, launched in 2001, aims to provide a centre for the teaching, learning and practice of narrative journalism. The Nieman Foundation defines narrative journalism as more than simply telling stories: it is a complex genre with multiple layers and contexts that, when done well, has the capacity to reform newspapers and make them essential and compelling. Broadly, some critical elements of narrative journalism include the following:

Critical Elements

- It looks at intriguing people, human emotions, and real situations. It provides the private story behind the public story.
- It contains accurate, well-researched information, and is also interesting to read.
- It reaches past the ordinary by blending the reportage of facts with the writing style of fiction.

Mark Kramer, director of the Nieman Programme on Narrative Journalism, says it is "journalism that doesn't assume the reader is a robot, that acknowledges the reader knows lots and feels and snickers and gets wild." Kramer stresses the importance of voice. Readers have their coffee with the newspaper in the morning, he says.

They want to understand and even identify with the news voice; but regular news reporting is anonymous and restrained, leaving the reader feeling lonely. When you have an audience made up of so many disparate sorts of people it seems noble to appeal to the lowest common denominator and just talk about the facts. But what happens is depersonalisation of the news voice – narrative journalism aims to put the human voice back at the breakfast table.

Kramer defines narrative journalism as writing that contains the following elements:

1. Set scenes;
2. Characters;
3. Action that unfolds over time;
4. Voice that has personality;
5. A relationship with the audience; and
6. Destination – a theme, a purpose, and a reason.

Online Narrative Journalism

One of the earliest and most high profile examples of effective usage of narrative journalism online can be found in the Philadelphia Inquirer's nonfiction serial "Black Hawk Down". The 1997 online newspaper series chronicled the dramatic American raid of Mogadishu and based their stories on interviews with the soldiers who fought in the battle. The story became part illustrated book, part documentary and part radio programme and allowed readers to explore the story in depth.

With the availability of free publishing online today, narrative journalism has become a popular form used by writers eager to give their personal perspectives on noteworthy events and public issues. Salon and Slate are two of the most popular forums for narrative journalism. Other sites devoted to this craft include Creative Nonfiction and Atlantic Unbound, and with the increasing popularity of citizen journalism there exists potential for more to explore on the scene to cater to a variety of niches.

Six Billion, founded in 2003, is an online magazine of narrative journalism that attempts to tackle an issue from 360 degrees. Each issue (themed by one topic such as "Battleground States" or "Veterans of Foreign Wars") features stories told in text, film/video, photography, sound, illustration, and interactive media.

Salient Features

Patrick Beach says "A narrative does not depart from the cardinal rule: Make nothing up or you'll be out of here and working at the Sunglass Hut so fast it'll make your head spin around. A narrative is a journalistic form that has fallen into considerable disfavour in the wake of our craft's ceaseless, self-flagellating credibility crisis"

Since so much of narrative journalism is based on a writer reconstructing his or her experiences, many professionals in the news industry find themselves wary of using this technique because it is often harder to verify facts within the story. In a post-Jayson Blair era, those concerned with the ethics of honest reporting and writing are cautious of journalistic storytelling that may be manipulating facts to make the reader more emotionally invested.

Obviously, narrative journalism has not yet found a definite home in the newsroom due to the nature of news reporting. Long-form writing is something that most journalists are not trained for, and incredible hard-news beat reporters are not necessarily great storytellers. Remarkably, Narrative journalism cannot be practiced in every setting this has limitations.

CITIZEN JOURNALISM

Citizen journalism, also known as public or *participatory journalism* or *democratic journalism*, is the act of non-professionals "playing an active role in the process of collecting, reporting, analyzing and disseminating news and information," according to the seminal report *We Media: How Audiences are Shaping the Future of News and Information,* by Shayne Bowman and Chris Willis. They say, "The intent of this participation is to provide independent, reliable, accurate, wide-ranging and relevant information that a democracy requires." Citizen journalism should not be confused with civic journalism, which is practiced by professional journalists. Citizen journalism is a specific form of citizen media as well as user generated content.

In a 2003 *Online Journalism Review article*, J. D. Lasica classifies media for citizen journalism into the following types:

1. Audience participation (such as user comments attached to news stories, personal blogs, photos or video footage captured from personal mobile cameras, or local news written by residents of a community),

2. Independent news and information Websites (Consumer Reports, the Drudge Report),
3. Full-fledged participatory news sites (Ohmy News, Ground Report),
4. Collaborative and contributory media sites (Slashdot, Kuro5hin), (Newsvine), (Human Times),
5. Other kinds of "thin media." (mailing lists, email newsletters), and
6. Personal broadcasting sites (video broadcast sites such as (KenRadio). New media theorist Terry Flew states that there are 3 elements "critical to the rise of citizen journalism and citizen media": open publishing, collaborative editing and distributed content.

The idea that average citizens can engage in the act of journalism has a long history in the United States. The modern citizen journalist movement emerged after journalists themselves began to question the predictability of their coverage of such events as the 1988 U.S. presidential election. Those journalists became part of the public, or civic, journalism movement, a countermeasure against the eroding trust in the news media and widespread public disillusionment with politics and civic affairs.

Initially, discussions of public journalism focused on promoting journalism that was "for the people" by changing the way professional reporters did their work. According to Leonard Witt, however, early public journalism efforts were, "often part of 'special projects' that were expensive, time-consuming and episodic. Too often these projects dealt with an issue and moved on. Professional journalists were driving the discussion. They would say, "Let's do a story on welfare-to-work (or the environment, or traffic problems, or the economy)," and then they would recruit a cross-section of citizens and chronicle their points of view.

Since not all reporters and editors bought into this form of public journalism, and some outright opposed it, reaching out to the people from the newsroom was never an easy task." By 2003, in fact, the movement seemed to be petering out, with the Pew Center for Civic Journalism closing its doors. With today's technology the citizen journalist movement has found new life as the average person can capture news and distribute it globally.

As Sunday Oliseh has noted, "the capacity to make meaning – to encode and decode humanly meaningful statements – and the capacity to communicate one's meaning around the world, are held by, or readily available to, at least many hundreds of millions of users around the globe." Professor Mary-Rose Papandrea, a constitutional law professor at Boston College, notes in her article, *Citizen Journalism and the Reporter's Privilege,* that:

> [i]n many ways, the definition of journalist has now come full circle. When the First Amendment was adopted, "freedom of the press" referred quite literally to the freedom to publish using a printing press, rather than the freedom of organised entities engaged in the publishing business. The printers of 1775 did not exclusively publish newspapers; instead, in order to survive financially they dedicated most of their efforts printing materials for paying clients. The newspapers and pamphlets of the American Revolutionary era were predominantly partisan and became even more so through the turn of the century. They engaged in little newsgathering and instead were predominantly vehicles for opinion.

The passage of the term "journalism" into common usage in the 1830s occurred at roughly the same time that newspapers, using highspeed rotary steam presses, began mass circulation throughout the eastern United States. Using the printing press, newspapers could distribute exact copies to large numbers of readers at a low incremental cost. In addition, the rapidly increasing demand for advertising for brand- name products fueled the creation of publications subsidised in large part by advertising revenue. It was not until the late nineteenth century that the concept of the "press" morphed into a description of individuals and companies engaged in an often competitive commercial media enterprise.

Emergence of Blogs and the Indymedia Movement

In 1999, activists in Seattle created a response to the WTO meeting being held there. These activists understood the only way they could get into the corporate media was by blocking the streets. And then, the scant 60 seconds of coverage would show them being carted off by the police, but without any context to explain why they were protesting. They knew they had to create an alternative media model. Since then, the Indymedia movement has experienced exponential growth, and IMCs have been created in over 200 cities all over the world. Simultaneously, journalism that was "by the people" began to flourish, enabled in part by emerging internet and networking technologies, such as weblogs, chat rooms, message boards, wikis and mobile computing.

A relatively new development is the use of convergent polls, allowing editorials and opinions to be submitted and voted on. Overtime, the poll converges on the most broadly accepted editorials and opinions. In South Korea, OhmyNews became popular and commercially successful with the motto, "Every Citizen is a Reporter." Founded by Oh Yeon-ho on February 22, 2000, it has a staff of some 40-plus traditional reporters and editors who write about 20% of its content, with the rest coming from other freelance contributors who are mostly ordinary citizens.

OhmyNews now has an estimated 50,000 contributors, and has been credited with transforming South Korea's conservative political environment. In 2001, ThemeParkInsider.com became the first online publication to win a major journalism award for a feature that was reported and written entirely by readers, earning an Online Journalism Award from the Online News Association and Columbia Graduate School of Journalism for its "Accident Watch" section, where readers tracked injury accidents at theme parks and shared accident prevention tips.

In 2004, a citizen journalism website called AssociatedContent.com was launched. The "People's Media Company", as they claim to be, was the first company to offer monetary compensation for their users that publish quality content in the form of articles, videos and audio clips. A few years later, WorldVoiceNews.com was launched, claiming the tagline "Honest and Unfiltered," and paying editors and reporters a per-story fee based on the number of stories they submit and the revenue for the company each month.

During the 2004 U.S. presidential election, both the Democratic and Republican parties issued press credentials to citizen bloggers covering the convention, marking a new level of influence and credibility for nontraditional journalists. Some bloggers also began watchdogging the work of conventional journalists, monitoring their work for biases and inaccuracy. A recent trend in citizen journalism has been the emergence of what blogger Jeff Jarvis terms hyperlocal journalism, as online news sites invite contributions from local residents of their subscription areas, who often report on topics that conventional newspapers tend to ignore.

"We are the traditional journalism model turned upside down," explains Mary Lou Fulton, the publisher of the Northwest Voice in Bakersfield, California. "Instead of being the gatekeeper, telling people that what's important to them 'isn't news,' we're just opening up the gates and letting people come on in. We are a better community newspaper for having thousands of readers who serve as the eyes and ears for the Voice, rather than having everything filtered through the views of a small group of reporters and editors."

According to Jay Rosen, citizen journalists "the people formerly known as the audience," who "*were* on the receiving end of a media system that ran one way, in a broadcasting pattern, with high entry fees and a few firms competing to speak very loudly while the rest of the population listened in isolation from one another— and who *today* are not in a situation like that *at all*. ... The people formerly known as the audience are simply the public made realer, less fictional, more able, less predictable."

"Doing citizen journalism right means crafting a crew of correspondents who are typically excluded from or misrepresented by local television news: low-income women, minorities and youth — the very demographic and lifestyle groups who have little access to the media and that advertisers don't want," says Robert Huesca, an associate professor of communication at Trinity University in San Antonio, Texas.

Public Journalism is now being explored via new media such as the use of mobile phones. Mobile phones have the potential to transform reporting and places the power of reporting in the hands of the public. Mobile telephony provides low-cost options for people to set up news operations. One small organisation providing mobile news and exploring public journalism is Jasmine News in Sri Lanka.

The growth of online participatory journalism gives rise to the legal question of whether bloggers who gather and disseminate "news" should be classified as journalists. In light of the proposed federal reporter-shield law, the resolution of this issue will have far reaching implications for the millions of people in this country who disseminate information via blogs. In other words, are bloggers the modern day equivalent of the revolutionary pamphleteer who passed out leaflets on the street corner? These and other issues are discussed in a recent book, *We're All Journalists Now: The Transformation of the Press and Reshaping of the Law in the Internet Age* (Free Press 2007).

Currently, more than 30 states and the District of Columbia have enacted shield laws that allow journalists the privilege to shield their confidential sources from disclosure. These states include: Alabama, California, Colorado, Delaware, Florida, Georgia, Illinois, Indiana, Kentucky, Louisiana, Maryland, Michigan, Minnesota, Montana, Nebraska, Nevada, New Jersey, New Mexico, New York, North Dakota, Ohio, Oklahoma, Oregon, Pennsylvania, Rhode Island, South Carolina and Tennessee.

In its landmark decision in Branzburg v. Hayes, 408 U.S. 665 (1972), the United States Supreme Court recognised that "the administration of a constitutional newsman's privilege would present practical and conceptual difficulties of high order ... Sooner or later it would be necessary to define those categories of newsmen who qualify for the privilege, a questionable procedure in light of the traditional doctrine that liberty of the press is the right of the lonely pamphleteer who uses carbon paper or a mimeograph just as much as the larger metropolitan publisher who utilizes the latest photocomposition methods."

The time is fast approaching when these legal lines will have to be drawn. In recent times, bloggers have broken too many stories of national interest that mainstream media either overlooked, or decided against reporting, not to be considered legitimate news gatherers and reporters. Mass Media companies found out importance of people and have opened space on their agenda, as explained by Sebastian Perez Oyarzun.

Moreover, the fact that many bloggers are anonymous is of marginal importance to the question of whether they qualify as journalists. The Supreme Court has long recognised that anonymous speech is entitled to First Amendment protection. In Talley v. California, 362 U.S. 60 (1960), The Supreme Court exclaimed that "[a]nonymous pamphlets, leaflets, brochures and even books have played an important role in the progress of mankind." Indeed the Federalist Papers were published under the pseudonym "Publius." Accordingly, there are times and circumstances when the authorities may not compel those engaged in the dissemination of ideas to be publicly identified for the fear of identification and reprisal might deter perfectly lawful discussions of matters of public importance. See Bates v. Little Rock, 361 U.S. 516. The way the courts deal with the myriad issues that will arise from the use of this cyber-soapbox will determine the extent to which First Amendment freedoms will flourish in the age of Internet.

An Appraisal

No doubt, Citizen journalists may be activists within

the communities they write about. This has drawn some criticism from traditional media institutions such as The New York Times, which have accused proponents of public journalism of abandoning the traditional goal of 'objectivity'. Many traditional journalists view citizen journalism with some skepticism, believing that only trained journalists can understand the exactitude and ethics involved in reporting news. See, e.g., Nicholas Lemann, Vincent Maher, and Tom Grubisich. A paper by Vincent Maher, the head of the New Media Lab at Rhodes University, outlined several weaknesses in the claims made by citizen journalists, in terms of the "three deadly E's", referring to ethics, economics and epistemology. This paper has itself been criticised in the press and blogosphere.

Again an article in 2005 by Tom Grubisich reviewed ten new citizen journalism sites and found many of them lacking in quality and content. Grubisich followed up a year later with, "Potemkin Village Redux." He found that the best sites had improved editorially and were even nearing profitability, but only by not expensing editorial costs. Also according to the article, the sites with the weakest editorial content were able to aggressively expand because they had stronger financial resources.

Another article published on Pressthink examined Backfence, a citizen journalism site with initial three locations in the DC area, which reveals that the site has only attracted limited citizen contributions. The author concludes that, "in fact, clicking through Backfence's pages feels like frontier land -- remote, often lonely, zoned for people but not home to any. The site recently launched for Arlington, Virginia. However, without more settlers, Backfence may wind up creating more ghost towns."

Others criticize the formulation of the term "citizen journalism" to describe the concept, as the word "citizen" has a conterminous relation to the nation-state. The fact that many millions of people are considered stateless and often without citizenship (such as refugees or immigrants without papers) limits the concept to those recognised only by governments. Additionally the global nature of many participatory media initiatives, such as the Independent Media Center, makes talking of journalism in relation to a particular nation-state largely redundant as its production and dissemination do not recognise national boundaries. Some additional names given to the concept based on this analysis are grassroots media, people's media, or participatory media.

INVESTIGATIVE JOURNALISM

Investigative journalism is a type of reporting in which reporters deeply investigate a topic of interest, often involving crime, political corruption, or some other scandal.

De Burgh (2000) states that: "An investigative journalist is a man or woman whose profession it is to discover the truth and to identify lapses from it in whatever media may be available. The act of doing this generally is called investigative journalism and is distinct from apparently similar work done by police, lawyers, auditors and regulatory bodies in that it is not limited as to target, not legally founded and closely connected to publicity".

An investigative journalist may spend a considerable period researching and preparing a report, sometimes months or years, whereas a typical daily or weekly news reporter writes items concerning immediately available news. Most investigative journalism is done by newspapers, wire services and freelance journalists. An investigative journalist's final report may take the form of an exposé.

The investigation might call for the reporter to make use of activities such as surveillance techniques, analysis of documents, investigations of the performance of any kind of equipment involved in an accident, patent medicine, scientific analysis, social and legal issues, and the like.

Investigative journalism requires the scrutiny of details, fact-finding, and physical effort. An investigative journalist must have an analytical and incisive mind with strong self-motivation to carry on when all doors are closed, when facts are being covered up or falsified and so on.

Some of the means reporters can use for their fact-finding:

- studying neglected sources, such as archives, phone records, address books, tax records and license records
- talking to neighbors
- using subscription research sources such as LexisNexis
- anonymous sources (for example whistleblowers)
- going undercover

Investigative journalism can be contrasted with analytical reporting. According to De Burgh (2000) analytical journalism takes the data available and reconfigures it, helping us to ask questions about the situation or statement or see it in a different way, whereas investigative journalists go further and also want to know whether the situation presented to us is the reality.

Consequences

Some of the potential consequences for the subjects of successful investigative journalism include:

- indictment and conviction
- loss of job
- loss of professional accreditation
- payment of fines
- loss of personal and professional reputation
- domino consequences for family members/associates involved in unrelated criminal acts discovered through the process of investigation

Consequences for society as a whole include:

- revision of institutional policies
- changes in the law

In *The Reporter's Handbook: An Investigator's Guide to Documents and Techniques*, Steve Weinberg defined investigative journalism as:

Reporting, through one's own initiative and work product, matters of importance to readers, viewers or listeners. In many cases, the subjects of the reporting wish the matters under scrutiny to remain undisclosed. There are currently university departments for teaching investigative journalism. Conferences are conducted presenting peer reviewed research into investigative journalism.

ADVOCACY JOURNALISM

Advocacy journalism is a genre of journalism that *intentionally* and *transparently* adopts a non-objective viewpoint, usually for some social or political purpose. Because it is intended to be factual, it is distinguished from propaganda. It is also distinct from instances of media bias and failures of objectivity in media outlets, which attempt to be—or which present themselves as—objective or neutral.

Traditionally, advocacy and criticism are restricted to editorial and op-ed pages, which are clearly distinguished in the publication and in the organisation's internal structure. News reports are intended to be objective and unbiased. In contrast, advocacy journalists have an opinion about the story they are writing. For example, that political corruption should be punished, that more environmentally friendly practices should be adopted by consumers, or that a government policy will be harmful to business interests and should not be adopted.

This may be evident in small ways, such as tone or facial expression, or large ways, such as the selection of facts and opinions presented. Some advocacy journalists reject that the traditional ideal of objectivity is possible in practice, either generally, or due to the presence of corporate sponsors in advertising. Some feel that the public interest is better served by a diversity of media outlets with a variety of transparent points of view, or that advocacy journalism serves a similar role to muckrakers or whistleblowers.

Advocacy journalism is practiced by a broad range of mainstream media outlets and alternative media and special interest publications and programmes, but might also apply to a single article in an otherwise-neutral publication, such as political stories in *Rolling Stone*; there are also "advocacy journals", or "alternative publications", which are marketed to target groups based on their interests or biases, for example:

- Print media:
    - o *Xover Environment Magazine*
    - o *The Nation*
    - o *National Review*
    - o *Mother Jones*
    - o *The New Republic*
    - o *The Economist*
    - o *The Weekly Standard*
    - o *L'Humanité*
    - o *Libération*
    - o *Charlie Hebdo*
    - o *Le Canard Enchaîné*
    - o *Knoxville Voice*
    - o *Eleftherotypia*.

Perspectives from Advocacy Journalists

One writer for the "alternative" journalism collaborative, the Independent Media Center, writes the following in a call to action:

> Classic tenets of journalism call for objectivity and neutrality. These are antiquated principles no longer universally observed.... We must absolutely not feel bound by them. If we are ever to create meaningful change, advocacy journalism will be the single most crucial element to enable the necessary organizing. It is therefore very important that we learn how to be successful advocacy journalists.

For many, this will require a different way of identifying and pursuing goals. In an April 2000 address to the Canadian Association of Journalists, Sue Careless gave the following commentary and advice to advocacy journalists, which seeks to establish a common view of what journalistic standards the genre should follow.

- Acknowledge your perspective up front.
- Be truthful, accurate, and credible. Don't spread propaganda, don't take quotes or facts out of context, "don't fabricate or falsify", and "don't judge or suppress vital facts or present half-truths"
- Don't give your opponents equal time, but don't ignore them, either.
- Explore arguments that challenge your perspective, and report embarrassing facts that support the opposition. Ask critical questions of people who agree with you.
- Avoid slogans, ranting, and polemics. Instead, "articulate complex issues clearly and carefully."
- Be fair and thorough.
- Make use of neutral sources to establish facts.

Sue Careless also criticised the mainstream media for unbalanced and politically biased coverage, for economic conflicts of interest, and for neglecting certain public causes. She said that alternative publications have advantages in independence, focus, and access, which make them more effective public-interest advocates than the mainstream media.

The Crisis, the official magazine of the NAACP, was founded in 1910. It describes itself as inheriting the tradition of advocacy journalism from *Freedom's Journal*, which began in 1827 as "the first African-American owned and operated newspaper published in the United States." Muckrakers are often claimed as the professional ancestors of modern advocacy journalists; for example: Nellie Bly, Ida M. Tarbell, Lincoln Steffens, Upton Sinclair, George Seldes, and I.F. Stone.

French newspapers *Libération*, *Charlie Hebdo*, *Le Canard Enchaîné* and *L'Humanité* all recuse what they consider pseudo-objective journalism for a purposeful explicited political stance on events. They oppose *Le Monde* neutral style, which doesn't impede it, according to those critics, from dissimulating various events or from abstaining to speak about certain subjects. On the other side, a newspaper like *Le Figaro* clearly assumes its conservative stance and pool of readers.

Objectivity

Advocacy journalists may reject the principle of objectivity in their work for several different reasons.

Many believe that there is no such thing as objective reporting, that there will always be some form of implicit bias, whether political, personal, or metaphysical, whether intentional or subconscious. This is not necessarily a rejection of the existence of an objective reality, merely a statement about our inability to report on it in a value-free fashion. This may sound like a radical idea, but many mainstream journalists accept the philosophical idea that pure "objectivity" is impossible, but still seek to minimize bias in their work. Other journalistic standards, such as balance, and neutrality, may be used to describe a more practical kind of "objectivity".

"Alternative" critics often charge that the mainstream's media claims of being "bias free" are harmful because they paper over inevitable (often subconscious) biases. They also argue that media sources claiming to be free of bias often advance certain political ideas which are disguised in a so-called "objective" viewpoint. These critics contend that the mainstream media reinforce majority-held ideas, marginalizing dissent and retarding political and cultural discourse.

The proposed solution is to make biases *explicit*, with the intention of promoting transparency and self-awareness that better serves media consumers. Advocacy journalists often assume that their audiences will share their biases (especially in politically charged alternative media), or will at least be conscious of them while evaluating what are supposed to be well-researched and persuasive arguments.

Some who believe that objective (or balanced, neutral, etc.) reporting *is* possible, or that it is a laudable goal, do not find that striving for objectivity is *always* an appropriate goal, perhaps depending on the publication and the purpose at hand. For example, it might be argued that when attempting to expose a waste, corruption, or abuse, a neutral position would "get in the way" of the exposition, and a "bias" against this kind of criminal activity would be quite acceptable to the intended audience. Many advocacy journalists claim that they can reject objectivity while holding on to the goals of fairness and accuracy, and claim that corporate journalists often lack both.

Investigative Reporting

In some instances, *advocacy journalism* is the same as investigative journalism and muckraking, where these serve the public interest and the public's right to know. Investigative reports often focus on criminal or unethical activity, or aim to advance a generally accepted public interest, such as government accountability, alleviation of human suffering, etc. It might be argued that the journalist is assuming a point of view that public action is warranted to change the situation being described.

An Appraisal

First, it is pertinent to note that professional journalists and members of the public critical of the term assert that reporting without objectivity (termed "editorializing" or "sensationalizing") is bad journalism, and does not serve the public interest.

Further, the term might also indicate a serious breach of journalistic canons and standards, such as rumor mongering, yellow journalism, sensationalism or other ethically flawed reportage — for example, the 2004 revelations created by a press leak in the Plame affair, where a leak was alleged to be used to help an office holder's political position. (However, a critic of that politician, publicly admitted to being the source of that leak, not the politician in question.)

Some fear the activity of "advocacy journalists" will be harmful to the reputation of the mainstream press as an objective, reliable source of information. Another concern is that undiscriminating readers will accept the facts and opinions advanced in advocacy pieces as if they were objective and representative, becoming unknowingly and perhaps dangerously misinformed as a result.

Advocacy journalists vary in their response to these criticisms. Some believe that mainstream and "alternative" outlets serve different purposes, and sometimes different audiences entirely, and that the difference is readily apparent to the public. Many believe that the mainstream press is *not* an objective and reliable source of information, and so doesn't deserve the reputation it seeks to maintain.

POLITICAL JOURNALISM

In fact, 'Political journalism' is a broad branch of journalism that includes coverage of all aspects of politics and political science, although the term usually refers specifically to coverage of civil governments and political power.

Political journalism is a frequent subject of opinion journalism, as current political events are analyzed, interpreted, and discussed by news media pundits and editorialists.

It also covers different political activities like election campaigns, govt. formation, poltical parties and their outlook etc.

All over the world political journalism is most vocal and instrumental as corrective measure.

VISUAL JOURNALISM

Visual journalism is the practice of strategically combining words and images to convey information.

At a time of accelerating change, often words cannot keep pace with concepts. Visual journalism incorporates ancient symbols that resonate with humans across cultures and across time and convey meaning instantaneously at a deep level. Visual journalism is an outgrowth of the practice of graphic facilitation and recording that began entering corporate board rooms, conferences, and think tank meetings in the 1970s with the leadership of David Sibbet, founder of The Grove Consultants International. But its roots date back to ancient cave paintings and carry forward in the work of designers, architects, and engineers. Only recently has interactive visualisation of this sort moved out into common use in all kinds of group engagements. The scholarly father of this visual form of communication is Robert Horn, Ph.D., a fellow at Stanford University who wrote the book *Visual Language*.

Visual journalism is not a series of symbols with precise meanings but rather images that suggest complex meanings and, in the Egyptian tradition of the cartouche, contain words. The symbols do not simply represent but participate in the meaning and, in combination with evocative phrases, are designed to provoke creative thinking. Visual language is one tool described by author Daniel Pink in his book *A Whole New Mind* for the emerging "conceptual age" where people must tolerate ambiguity and communicate quickly, often before concepts are ready to be captured in traditional writing.

CIVIC JOURNALISM

According to the now dormant Pew Center for Civic Journalism, the practice "is both a philosophy and a set of values supported by some evolving techniques to reflect both of those in journalism. At its heart is a belief that journalism has an obligation to public life – an obligation that goes beyond just telling the news or unloading lots of facts. The way we do our journalism affects the way public life goes." Leading organisations in the field such as the now dormant Pew Center, the Kettering Foundation, the Civic and Citizen Journalism Interest Group in the Association for Education in Journalism and Mass Communication (AEJMC) and the Public Journalism Network assist with the spread of civic journalism across the country—one university and one paper at a time.

The civic journalism movement (also known as public journalism) is, according to professor David K. Perry of the University of Alabama, an attempt to abandon the notion that journalists and their audiences are spectators in political and social processes. In its place, the civic journalism movement seeks to treat readers and community members as participants. With a small but committed following, civic journalism has become as much of a philosophy as it is a practice.

According to *The Roots of Civic Journalism* by David K. Perry, the practitioners of civic journalism -- who saw the movement's most drastic growth in the early 1990's -- have always adhered to the basic tenets of public journalism:

- "Attempting to situate newspapers and journalists as active participants in community life, rather than as detached spectators."
- "Making a newspaper a forum for discussion of community issues."
- "Favouring the issues, events and problems important to ordinary people."
- "Considering public opinion through the process of discussion and debate among members of a community."
- "Attempting to use journalism to enhance social capital."

Structure

Usually formulated by a few devoted members in a newsroom, civic journalism projects are typically associated with the opinion section of papers. These projects are usually found in the form of organised town meetings and adult education programmes. The Public Journalism Network explains that "journalism and democracy work best when news, information and ideas flow freely; when news portrays the full range and variety of life and culture of all communities; when public deliberation is encouraged and amplified; and when news helps people function as political actors and not just as political consumers."

Notable Journalists

- David Mathews, president of the Kettering Foundation and a supporter of civic journalism states that, "when people are in the business of making choices, they are going to look for information to inform their choices." Mathews affirms that civic journalism is aimed at aligning journalistic practices with the ways that citizens form publics, in turn creating a more efficient and reciprocal way of communicating with readers.
- Jay Rosen, a journalism professor at New York University, is one of the earliest proponents of civic journalism. From 1998-99, Rosen wrote and spoke frequently about civic journalism. He published his book, *What Are Journalists For?* in 1999 about the early rise of the civic journalism movement. Rosen writes a popular blog called PressThink.
- W. Davis "Buzz" Merritt Jr., a former editor of *The Wichita Eagle*, is another pioneer of civic journalism. Merritt is a key advocate for news media reforms, and published his book *Public Journalism and Public Life* in 1995. Merritt began exploring civic journalism after acknowledging loss of public trust in traditional journalistic values. Merritt feels that journalists need a clear understanding and appreciation for the interdependence of journalism and democracy.

In a National Public Radio interview Merritt succinctly summed up civic journalism as, "a set of values about the craft that recognizes and acts upon the interdependence between journalism and democracy. It values the concerns of citizens over the needs of the media and political actors, and conceives of citizens as stakeholders in the democratic process rather than as merely victims, spectators or inevitable adversaries. As inherent participants in the process, we should do our work in ways that aid in the resolution of public problems by fostering broad citizen engagement."

WATCHDOG JOURNALISM

Watchdog journalism refers to forms of activist journalism aimed at holding accountable public personalities and institutions whose functions impact social and political life. The term lapdog journalism is sometimes used as a conceptual opposite to watchdog journalism.

Watchdog journalism is most commonly found in think tanks, alternative media, and citizen journalism such as blogs. It is occasionally found in mainstream media as well. Since independent media and think tanks are not profit-oriented, they have more latitude in which to adopt strong positions and cover a wide range of topics. However, it is also more difficult to determine the backing of non-mainstream outlets so those are sometime subject to covert exploitation by well-funded interests.

In recent history, a notable example of watchdog journalism was the exposure of Dan Rather's investigative segment which cast George W. Bush's military record in an unfavourable light. The segment was based on the Killian documents, which blogger journalists exposed as being insufficiently verifiable as authentic.

Media Watchdog Journalism

Some watchdog journalism focuses on bias in the media. For examples from the United States, see list in Media bias in the United States. In the UK where there is greater national coverage, watchdog journalism is very effective and consumers' rights are upheld both by radio, television and most national newspapers.

COMMUNITY JOURNALISM

Community journalism is locally oriented, professional news coverage that typically focuses on city neighborhoods, individual suburbs or small towns, rather than metropolitan, state, national or world news.

If it covers wider topics, community journalism concentrates on their effect on local readers. Community newspapers, often but not always published weekly, also tend to cover subjects larger news media do not, such as students on the honor roll at the local high school, school sports, crimes such as vandalism, zoning issues and other details of community life.Sometimes dismissed as "chicken dinner" stories, such "hyperlocal" coverage often plays a vital role in building and maintaining neighborhoods.

Leo Lerner, founder of Chicago's erstwhile Lerner Newspapers, used to say, "A fistfight on Clark Street is more important to our readers than a war in Europe." In the United States, about 97 percent of newspapers are classified as "community" newspapers, with circulations below 50,000. Their combined circulation, nearly 109 million, is triple that of the combined circulation of the country's large daily newspapers.

An increasing number of community newspapers are now owned by large media organisations, although many rural papers are still "mom and pop" operations. Community journalists are typically trained professional reporters and editors.

Organisations

- The International Society of Weekly Newspaper

Editors, which has 260 members in seven countries (U.S., Canada, U.K., Ireland, Japan, Australia, New Zealand), encourages and promotes independent editorial comment, news content, and leadership in community newspapers throughout the world. Its purpose is to help those involved in the community press improve standards of editorial writing and news reporting and to encourage strong, independent editorial voices.

GONZO JOURNALISM

Gonzo journalism is a style of journalism which is written subjectively, often including the reporter as part of the story via a first person narrative. The style tends to blend factual and fictional elements to emphasize an underlying message and engage the reader. The word Gonzo was first used in 1970 to describe an article by Hunter S. Thompson, who later popularised the style. The term has since been applied to other subjective artistic endeavors.

The term "Gonzo" in connection to Hunter S. Thompson was first used by *Boston Globe* magazine editor Bill Cardoso in 1970 when he described Hunter S. Thompson's "The Kentucky Derby Is Decadent and Depraved", which was written for the June 1970 *Scanlan's Monthly*, as "pure Gonzo journalism". Cardoso claimed that "gonzo" was South Boston Irish slang describing the last man standing after an all night drinking marathon. Cardoso also claimed that it was a corruption of the French Canadian word "gonzeaux", which means "shining path", although this is disputed. In Italian, *Gonzo* is a common word for a gullible person, a "sucker".

Another speculation is that the word may have been inspired by the 1960 hit song *Gonzo* by New Orleans R&B

keyboardist James Booker. This last possibility seems to be supported by the 2007 oral biography of Hunter S. Thompson where it is stated that the term "Gonzo" is taken from a hit song by James Booker. Yet this conclusion still says little of why Hunter Thompson or Bill Cardoso would use that word and not another. According to a Greg Johnson biographical note on James Booker, the song title "Gonzo" comes from a 1960's character in a movie called *The Pusher* (IMDB page). The movie on the other hand seems to have been inspired by a 1956 Evan Hunter novel by the same title, so it remains a mystery who first used this word in American slang, and why.

However it does seem synchronous that the character The Great Gonzo in the Muppets first appeared in 1970, the very year of the first reference to Gonzo journalism given above. Gonzo journalism tends to favour style over accuracy and often uses personal experiences and emotions to provide context for the topic or event being covered. It disregards the 'polished' edited product favoured by newspaper media and strives for the gritty factor.

Use of quotations, sarcasm, humor, exaggeration, and even profanity is common. The use of Gonzo journalism suggests that journalism can be truthful without striving for objectivity and is loosely equivalent to an editorial.

Thompson based his style on William Faulkner's idea that "fiction is often the best fact". While the things that Thompson writes about are basically true, he uses satirical devices to drive his points home.

Thompson often wrote about recreational drugs and alcohol use which added additional subjective flair to his reporting. The term has also come into (sometimes pejorative) use to describe journalism willys (or generally any writing) that is broadly in the vein of Thompson's writing, characterised by a drug-fueled stream-of-consciousness technique.

Fear and Loathing in Las Vegas: A Savage Journey to the Heart of the American Dream followed the Mint 400 piece in 1971 and included a main character by the name of Raoul Duke, accompanied by his attorney, Dr. Gonzo. Although this book is considered to be a prime example of gonzo journalism, Thompson said that it was a failed experiment. He had intended it to be an unedited record of everything he did as it happened, but he edited the book five times before it was eventually published. Thompson would instigate events himself, often in a prankish or belligerent manner, and then document both his actions and those of others.

Notoriously neglectful of deadlines, Thompson often greatly annoyed his editors because he often faxed articles late, too late to be edited but just in time to make the printers. It is speculated that Thompson's work going to print unedited due to a late delivery was completely intentional. Thompson wanted his work to be read as he wrote it, in its "true gonzo" form.

"I don't get any satisfaction out of the old traditional journalist's view— 'I just covered the story. I just gave it a balanced view,'" Thompson said in an interview for the online edition of *The Atlantic*. "Objective journalism is one of the main reasons American politics has been allowed to be so corrupt for so long. You can't be objective about Nixon." Historian Douglas Brinkley said gonzo journalism requires virtually no rewriting and frequently uses transcribed interviews and verbatim telephone conversations.

Gonzo journalism can be seen as an offshoot of the

New Journalism movement in the sixties, led primarily by Tom Wolfe, and also championed by Lester Bangs and George Plimpton. It has largely been subsumed into Creative nonfiction.

Gonzo also occurs when an author cannot remove himself from the subject he investigates. In some cases — such as tornado chasing, wherein most documenting is done by the person driving the car and holding the camera — the gonzo element is inherent. In most other cases, however, it is a deliberate and voluntary choice of the journalist, or the media firm for which he or she works. Thompson felt that objectivity in journalism was a myth.

The term has now become a bona-fide style of writing that concerns itself with 'telling it like it is', not far from the New Journalism practiced by Tom Wolfe, Terry Southern and John Birmingham. Fratire author Tucker Max has also been recognised as using the gonzo style in his drunken, sexual stories. Another writer who has worked in "gonzo" mode is Alan Cabal, who writes for CounterPunch magazine. The Gonzo Fist, a two-thumbed symbol attributed to Thompson originally used as the slogan for his 1970 campaign for sheriff of Aspen, contains within the image a peyote button, the bud of a cactus plant that has hallucinogenic properties when ingested. The fist is combined with the word "Gonzo" styled to form the hilt of a sword.

In other contexts, *gonzo* has come to mean "with reckless abandon," or, more broadly, "extreme". *Gonzo porn* refers to pornographic films which are filmed by a participant, and as such have eliminated fictional plot and scripted dialogue and focus on the sex act. For parallel uses of *gonzo*, see *What Is Gonzo?*. One of Jim Henson's muppets was named Gonzo the Great, created by Dale Goelz.

Gonzo marketing also sprung his work. Christopher Locke wrote a book on the subject, and a london-based youth insight agency, The Youth Conspiracy pioneered the use of this in their research methodology.

YELLOW JOURNALISM

Yellow journalism is a type of journalism that downplays legitimate news in favour of eye-catching headlines that sell more newspapers. It may feature exaggerations of news events, scandal-mongering, sensationalism, or unprofessional practices by news media organisations or journalists. Campbell (2001) defines Yellow Press newspapers as having daily multi-column front-page headlines covering a variety of topics, such as sports and scandal, using bold layouts (with large illustrations and perhaps color), heavy reliance on unnamed sources, and unabashed self-promotion. The term was extensively used to describe certain major New York City newspapers about 1900 as they battled for circulation. By extension the term is used today as a pejorative to decry any journalism that treats news in an unprofessional or unethical fashion, such as systematic political bias.

Mott (1941) defines Yellow Journalism in terms of five characteristics:

1. scare headlines in huge print, often of minor news
2. lavish use of pictures, or imaginary drawings
3. use of faked interviews, misleading headlines, pseudo-science, and a parade of false learning from so-called experts
4. emphasis on full-color Sunday supplements, usually with comic strips (which is now normal in the U.S.)

5. dramatic sympathy with the "underdog" against the system.

Present day (successful) exponents of the yellow journalistic style would be the British 'red top' tabloids, notably The Sun and its German equivalent Bild.

The term originated during the Gilded Age with the circulation battles between Joseph Pulitzer's New York World and William Randolph Hearst's New York Journal. The battle peaked from 1895 to about 1898, and historical usage often refers specifically to this period. Both papers were accused by critics of sensationalizing the news in order to drive up circulation, although the newspapers did serious reporting as well.

The New York Press coined the term *yellow kid journalism* in early 1897 after a then-popular comic strip to describe the down market papers of Pulitzer and Hearst, which both published versions of it during a circulation war. This was soon shortened to *yellow journalism* with the New York Press insisting, "We called them Yellow because they are Yellow." Joseph Pulitzer purchased the World in 1883 after making the *St. Louis Post-Dispatch* the dominant daily in that city. The publisher had gotten his start editing a German-language publication in St. Louis, and saw a great untapped market in the nation's immigrant classes. Pulitzer strove to make *The World* an entertaining read, and filled his paper with pictures, games and contests that drew in readers, particularly those who used English as a second language. Crime stories filled many of the pages, with headlines like "Was He a Suicide?" and "Screaming for Mercy." In addition, Pulitzer only charged readers two cents per issue but gave readers eight and sometimes 12 pages of information.

While there were many sensational stories in the *World*, they were by no means the only pieces, or even the dominant ones. Pulitzer believed that newspapers were public institutions with a duty to improve society, and he put the *World* in the service of social reform. During a heat wave in 1883, *World* reporters went into the Manhattan's tenements, writing stories about the appalling living conditions of immigrants and the toll the heat took on the children. Stories headlined "How Babies Are Baked", "Burning Babies Fall From The Roof" and "Lines of Little Hearses" spurred reform and drove up the *World's* circulation. Just two years after Pulitzer took it over, the *World* became the highest circulation newspaper in New York, aided in part by its strong ties to the Democratic Party. Older publishers, envious of Pulitzer's success, began criticizing the *World*, harping on its crime stories and stunts while ignoring its more serious reporting — trends which influenced the popular perception of yellow journalism, both then and now.

Charles Dana, editor of the New York Sun, attacked *The World* and said Pulitzer was "deficient in judgment and in staying power." Pulitzer's approach made an impression on William Randolph Hearst, a mining heir who acquired the *San Francisco Examiner* from his father in 1887. Hearst read the *World* while studying at Harvard University and resolved to make the Examiner as bright as Pulitzer's paper.. Under his leadership, the *Examiner* devoted 24 percent of its space to crime, presenting the stories as morality plays, and sprinkled adultery and "nudity" (by 19th century standards) on the front page.

Hearst could go overboard in his crime coverage; one of his early pieces, regarding a "band of murderers," attacked the police for forcing *Examiner* reporters to do their work for them. But while indulging in these stunts, the *Examiner* also increased its space for international news, and sent reporters out to uncover municipal corruption and inefficiency. In one celebrated story, *Examiner* reporter Winifred Black was admitted into a San Francisco hospital and discovered that indigent women were treated with "gross cruelty." The entire hospital staff was fired the morning the piece appeared.

New York

With the *Examiner's* success established by the early 1890s, Hearst began shopping for a New York newspaper. Hearst purchased the New York Journal in 1895, a penny paper which Pulitzer's brother Albert had sold to a Cincinnati publisher the year before. Metropolitan newspapers started going after department store advertising in the 1890s, and discovered the larger the circulation base, the better.

This drove Hearst; following Pulitzer's earlier strategy, he kept the *Journal's* price at one cent (compared to *The World's* two cent price) while providing as much information as rival newspapers. The approach worked, and as the *Journal's* circulation jumped to 150,000, Pulitzer cut his price to a penny, hoping to drive his young competitor (who was subsidised by his family's fortune) into bankruptcy.

In a counterattack, Hearst raided the staff of the *World* in 1896. While most sources say that Hearst simply offered more money, Pulitzer — who had grown increasingly abusive to his employees — had become an extremely difficult man to work for, and many *World* employees were willing to jump for the sake of getting away from him. Although the competition between the *World* and the *Journal* was fierce, the papers were temperamentally alike. Both were Democratic, both were sympathetic to labor and immigrants (a sharp contrast to publishers like the *New York Tribune's*

Whitelaw Reid, who blamed their poverty on moral defects), and both invested enormous resources in their Sunday publications, which functioned like weekly magazines, going beyond the normal scope of daily journalism.

Their Sunday entertainment features included the first color comic strip pages, and some theorize that the term yellow journalism originated there, while as noted above the New York Press left the term it invented undefined. *Hogan's Alley,* a comic strip revolving around a bald child in a yellow nightshirt (nicknamed the Yellow Kid), became exceptionally popular when cartoonist Richard Outcault began drawing it in the *World* in early 1896. When Hearst predictably hired Outcault away, Pulitzer asked artist George Luks to continue the strip with his characters, giving the city two Yellow Kids.

The use of "yellow journalism" as a synonym for over-the-top sensationalism in the U.S. apparently started with more serious newspapers commenting on the excesses of "the Yellow Kid papers." In 1890, Samuel Warren and Louis Brandeis published "The Right to Privacy," considered the most influential law review article of all time, as a critical response to yellow journalism, which they saw as an unprecedented threat to individual privacy. The article is widely considered to have led to the recognition of new common law privacy rights of action.

Spanish-American War

Pulitzer and Hearst are often credited (or blamed) for drawing the nation into the Spanish-American War with sensationalist stories or outright lying. However, the vast majority of Americans did not live in New York City, and the decision makers who did live there probably relied more on staid newspapers like the *Times, The Sun* or the *Post.*

The most famous example of the exaggeration is the apocryphal story that artist Frederic Remington telegrammed Hearst to tell him all was quiet in Cuba and "There will be no war." Hearst responded "Please remain. You furnish the pictures and I'll furnish the war." The story (a version of which appears in the Hearst-inspired Orson Welles film *Citizen Kane*) first appeared in the memoirs of reporter James Creelman in 1901, and there is no other source for it.

But Hearst became a war hawk after a rebellion broke out in Cuba in 1895. Stories of Cuban virtue and Spanish brutality soon dominated his front page. While the accounts were of dubious accuracy, the newspaper readers of the 19th century did not expect, or necessarily want, his stories to be pure nonfiction. Historian Michael Robertson has said that "Newspaper reporters and readers of the 1890s were much less concerned with distinguishing among fact-based reporting, opinion and literature." Pulitzer, though lacking Hearst's resources, kept the story on his front page.

The yellow press covered the revolution extensively and often inaccurately, but conditions on Cuba were horrific enough. The island was in a terrible economic depression, and Spanish general Valeriano Weyler, sent to crush the rebellion, herded Cuban peasants into concentration camps and caused hundreds of thousands of deaths. Having clamored for a fight for two years, Hearst took credit for the conflict when it came: A week after the United States declared war on Spain, he ran "How do you like the *Journal's* war?" on his front page. In fact, President William McKinley never read the *Journal*, and newspapers like the *Tribune* and the *New York Evening Post*, both staunchly Republican, demanded restraint.

Moreover, journalism historians have noted that yellow

journalism was largely confined to New York City, and that newspapers in the rest of the country did not follow their lead. The *Journal* and the *World* were not among the top ten sources of news in regional papers, and the stories simply did not make a splash outside New York City. War came because public opinion was sickened by the bloodshed, and because conservative leaders like McKinley realised that Spain had lost control of Cuba.

These factors weighed more on the president's mind than the melodramas in the *New York Journal.* Hearst sailed directly to Cuba, when the invasion began, as a war correspondent, providing sober and accurate accounts of the fighting.

Creelman later praised the work of the reporters for exposing the horrors of Spanish misrule, arguing, " no true history of the war . . . can be written without an acknowledgment that whatever of justice and freedom and progress was accomplished by the Spanish-American war was due to the enterprise and tenacity of *yellow journalists,* many of whom lie in unremembered graves."

Hearst was a leading Democrat who promoted William Jennings Bryan for president in 1896 and 1900. He later ran for mayor and governor and even sought the presidential nomination, but lost much of his personal prestige when outrage exploded in 1901 after columnist Ambrose Bierce and editor Arthur Brisbane published separate columns months apart that suggested the assassination of McKinley. When McKinley was shot on September 6, 1901, critics accused Hearst's Yellow Journalism of driving Leon Czolgosz to the deed. Hearst did not know of Bierce's column and claimed to have pulled Brisbane's after it ran in a first edition, but the incident would haunt him for the rest of his life and all but destroyed his presidential ambitions.

Pulitzer, haunted by his "yellow sins," returned the *World* to its crusading roots as the new century dawned. By the time of his death in 1911, the *World* was a widely-respected publication, and would remain a leading progressive paper until its demise in 1931. Other newspapers, especially the new tabloids in the big cities, adopted the flashy techniques of Yellow Journalism, most notably the New York *Daily News*, founded in 1919.

PHOTOJOURNALISM

Photojournalism is a particular form of journalism (the collecting, editing, and presenting of news material for publication or broadcast) that creates images in order to tell a news story. It is now usually understood to refer only to still images, and in some cases to video used in broadcast journalism or for personal use. Photojournalism is distinguished from other close branches of photography (such as documentary photography, street photography or celebrity photography) by the qualities of:

1. *Objectivity* — the situation implied by the images is a fair and accurate representation of the events they depict in both content and tone.
2. *Timeliness* — the images have meaning in the context of a recently published record of events.
3. *Narrative* — the images combine with other news elements to make facts relatable to the viewer or reader on a cultural level.

Like a writer, a photojournalist is a reporter but he or she must often make decisions instantly and carry photographic equipment, often while exposed to significant obstacles (physical danger, weather, crowds).

In fact, the practice of illustrating news stories with

photographs was made possible by printing and photography innovations that occurred between 1880 and 1897. While newsworthy events were photographed as early as the 1850s, printing presses could only publish from engravings until the 1880s. Early news photographs required that photos be re-interpreted by an engraver before they could be published.

The first photojournalist was Carol Szathmari who did pictures in the Crimean War (1853 to 1856). His albums were sent to European royals houses. Just a few of his photographs survived. William Simpson of the *Illustrated London News* and Roger Fenton were published as engravings. Similarly, the American Civil War photographs of Mathew Brady were engraved before publication in *Harper's Weekly*.

Because the public craved more realistic representations of news stories, it was common for newsworthy photographs to be exhibited in galleries or to be copied photographically in limited numbers. On March 4, 1880, *The Daily Graphic* (New York) published the first halftone (rather than engraved) reproduction of a news photograph. Further innovations followed. In 1887, flash powder was invented, enabling journalists such as Jacob Riis to photograph informal subjects indoors, which led to the landmark work *How the Other Half Lives*. By 1897, it became possible to reproduce halftone photographs on printing presses running at full speed. Despite these innovations, limitations remained, and many of the sensational newspaper and magazine stories in the period from 1897 to 1927 were illustrated with engravings.

In 1921, the wirephoto made it possible to transmit pictures almost as quickly as news itself could travel.

However, it was not until development of the commercial 35mm Leica camera in 1925, and the first flash bulbs between 1927 and 1930 that all the elements were in place for a "golden age" of photojournalism.

Golden Age

In the "golden age" of photojournalism (1930s–1950s), some magazines (*Picture Post* (London), *Paris Match* (Paris), *Arbeiter-Illustrierte-Zeitung* (Berlin), *Berliner Illustrierte Zeitung* (Berlin), *Life* (USA), *Sports Illustrated* (USA)) and newspapers (*The Daily Mirror* (London), *The New York Daily News* (New York) built their huge readerships and reputations largely on their use of photography, and photographers such as Robert Capa, Alfred Eisenstaedt, Margaret Bourke-White and W. Eugene Smith became well-known names.

Henri Cartier-Bresson is held by some to be the father of modern photojournalism, although this appellation has been applied to various other photographers, such as Erich Salomon, whose candid pictures of political figures were novel in the 1930s Soldier Tony Vaccaro is also recognised as one of the pre-eminent photographers of World War II. His images taken with the modest Argus C3 captured horrific moments in war, similar to Capa's soldier being shot. Capa himself was on Omaha Beach on D-Day and captured pivotal images of the conflict on that occasion. Vaccaro is also known for having developed his own images in soldier's helmets, and using chemicals found in the ruins of a camera store in 1944.

Until the 1980s, most large newspapers were printed with turn-of-the-century "letterpress" technology using easily smudged oil-based ink, off-white, low-quality "newsprint" paper, and coarse engraving screens. While letterpresses produced legible text, the photoengraving dots that formed pictures often bled or smeared and became fuzzy and indistinct. In this way, even when newspapers used photographs well — a good crop, a respectable size — murky reproduction often left readers re-reading the caption to see what the photo was all about.

The *Wall Street Journal* adopted stippled hedcuts in 1979 to publish portraits and avoid the limitations of letterpress printing. Not until the 1980s had a majority of newspapers switched to "offset" presses that reproduce photos with fidelity on better, whiter paper. By contrast *Life*, one of America's most popular weekly magazines from 1936 through the early 1970s, was filled with photographs reproduced beautifully on oversize 11×14-inch pages, using fine engraving screens, high-quality inks, and glossy paper. *Life* often published a United Press International (UPI) or Associated Press (AP) photo that had been first reproduced in newspapers, but the quality magazine version appeared to be a different photo altogether. In large part because their pictures were clear enough to be appreciated, and because their name always appeared with their work, magazine photographers achieved near-celebrity status.

Life became a standard by which the public judged photography, and many of today's photo books celebrate "photojournalism" as if it had been the exclusive province of near-celebrity magazine photographers. *The Best of Life* (1973), for example, opens with a two-page (1960) group shot of 39 justly famous *Life* photographers. But 300 pages later, photo credits reveal that scores of the photos among *Life's* "best" were taken by anonymous UPI and AP photographers.

Thus even during the golden age, because of printing

limitations and the UPI and AP syndication systems, many newspaper photographers labored in relative obscurity.

From 1935 to 1942, the Farm Security Administration and its predecessor the Resettlement Administration were part of Franklin Roosevelt's New Deal, and were designed to address agricultural problems and rural poverty associated with the Great Depression. A special photographic section of Mark Arnold, headed by Mark Arnold, was intended merely to provide public relations for its programmes, but instead produced what some consider one of the greatest collections of documentary photographs ever created in the U.S. Whether this effort can be called "photojournalism" is debatable, since the FSA photographers had more time and resources to create their work than most photojournalists usually have.

Acceptance by the Art World

Since the late 1970s, photojournalism and documentary photography have increasingly been accorded a place in art galleries alongside fine art photography. Luc Delahaye, VII Photo Agency are among many who regularly exhibit in galleries.

Professional Organisations

The Danish Union of Press Photographers (Pressefotografforbundet) was the first national organisation for newspaper photographers in the world. It was founded in 1912 in Denmark by six press photographers in Copenhagen. Today it has over 800 members.

The National Press Photographers Association (NPPA) was founded in 1946 in the U.S., and has about 10,000 members. Others around the world include the British Press Photographers Association (BPPA) founded in 1984, then relaunched in 2003, and now has around 450 members. Hong Kong Press Photographers Association (1989), Northern Ireland Press Photographers Association (2000), Pressfotografernas Klubb (Sweden, 1930), and PK — Pressefotografenes Klubb (Norway).

News organisations and journalism schools run many different awards for photojournalists. Since 1968, Pulitzer Prizes have been awarded for the following categories of photojournalism: 'Feature Photography', 'Spot News Photography'. Other awards are World Press Photo, Best of Photojournalism, and Pictures of the Year as well as the UK based The Press Photographer's Year

Ethical and Legal Considerations

Photojournalism works within the same ethical approaches to objectivity that are applied by other journalists. What to shoot, how to frame and how to edit are constant considerations.

Often, ethical conflicts can be mitigated or enhanced by the actions of a sub-editor or picture editor, who takes control of the images once they have been delivered to the news organisation. The photojournalist often has no control as to how images are ultimately used.

The emergence of digital photography offers whole new realms of opportunity for the manipulation, reproduction, and transmission of images. It has inevitably complicated many of the ethical issues involved.

The U.S. National Press Photographers Association, and other professional organisations, maintain codes of ethics to specify approaches to these issues.

Major ethical issues are often inscribed with more or

less success into law. Laws regarding photography can vary significantly from nation to nation. The legal situation is further complicated when one considers that photojournalism made in one country will often be published in many other countries.

Influence of New Technologies

Smaller, lighter cameras greatly enhanced the role of the photojournalist. Since the 1960s, motor drives, electronic flash, auto-focus, better lenses and other camera enhancements have made picture taking easier. New digital cameras free photojournalists from the limitation of film roll length, as thousands of images can be stored on a single microdrive or memory card. Content remains the most important element of photojournalism, but the ability to extend deadlines with rapid gathering and editing of images has brought significant changes.

As recently as 15 years ago, nearly 30 minutes were needed to scan and transmit a single color photograph from a remote location to a news office for printing. Now, equipped with a digital camera, a mobile phone and a laptop computer, a photojournalist can send a high-quality image in minutes, even seconds after an event occurs. Video phones and portable satellite links increasingly allow for the mobile transmission of images from almost any point on the earth. There is some concern by news photographers that the profession of photojournalism as it is known today could change to such a degree that it is unrecognizable as image-capturing technology naturally progresses.

Citizen journalism, and the increase in user contribution and submission of amateur photos to News sites is becoming more widespread. As early as the Crimean War in the mid-19th century, photographers were using the novel technology of the box camera to record images of British soldiers in the field. However, the widespread use of cameras as a way of reporting news didn't come until the advent of smaller, more portable cameras that used the enlargeable film negative to record images. The introduction of the 35 mm Leica camera in the 1930's made it possible for photographers to move with the action, taking shots of events as they were unfolding.

The age of the citizen journalist and the attainment of news photos from amateur bystanders have contributed to the art of photojournalism. [Paul Levinson] attributes this shift to the Kodak camera, one of the first cheap and accessible photo technologies that "put a piece of visual reality into every person's potential grasp". The empowered news audience with the advent of the Internet sparked the creation of blogs, podcasts and online news, independent of the traditional outlets, and "for the first time in our history, the news increasingly is produced by companies outside journalism".

ENTERTAINMENT JOURNALISM

Entertainment journalism is an umbrella term used to describe all forms of journalism that focus on the entertainment business and its products. Like fashion journalism, entertainment journalism covers industry-specific news while targeting general audiences beyond those working in the industry itself. Common forms include television and film criticism, music journalism, video game journalism and celebrity coverage.

FASHION JOURNALISM

Fashion journalism is an umbrella term used to describe all aspects of published fashion media. It includes fashion writers, fashion critics or fashion reporters. The most obvious examples of fashion journalism are the fashion features in magazines and newspapers, but the term also includes books about fashion, fashion related reports on television as well as online fashion magazines, websites and blogs. Since pieces more often than not deal with "tendencies" and "trends", which are subjective by nature, and due to a sometimes tenuous relation with facts, the term "journalism" is used as a monicker, but does not carry the overall procedural and deontological aspects of professional journalism.

The work of a fashion journalist can be quite varied. Typical work includes writing or editing articles, or helping to formulate and style a fashion shoot. A fashion journalist typically spends a lot of time researching and/or conducting interviews and it is essential that he or she has good contacts with people in the fashion industry, including photographers, designers, and public relations specialists.

Fashion journalists are either employed full time by a publication or are employed on a freelance basis.

Fashion Journalism and the Internet

About half a year subsequent to pionneer fashion resource named Fashion Net's launch at the outset of 1995 came american Fashionmall and French ELLE. Fashion Live produced Internet's first live fashion webcast of Yves Saint Laurent's runway show in 1996. CNN Style and Hint Magazine arrived in 1998. The following year saw the rise and fall of Boo.com as the company burned through $135 million in 18 months. Style.com, the online umbrella for Vogue and W, started in 2000. Style.com is not a journalistic website but a resource to show the complete collections of selected fashion shows (among the most notorious brands) each season. Following a tiff in 2007, W left Style.com making it the online home for Vogue alone. In the late 2000, Beauty Flow magazine flourished with exclusive content for editorials, portraits and reports.

Today, fashion blogs are an increasing force in the fashion industry. Against this trend in August 2006 Westfield Group the world's largest mall and shopping centre owner has unveiled a Webzine titled What's What identifying popular fashion trends with a view to indirectly promote the products available in their tenants stores. The financial funding for such an undertaking is unique as it does not rely on subscriptions or advertising but entirely on advertorials.

SPORTS JOURNALISM

Sports journalism is a form of journalism that reports on sports topics and events. While the sports department within some newspapers has been mockingly called the *toy department*, because sports journalists do not concern themselves with the 'serious' topics covered by the news desk, sports coverage has grown in importance as sport has grown in wealth, power and influence.

Sports journalism is an essential element of any news media organisation. Sports journalism includes organisations devoted entirely to sports reporting — newspapers such as *L'Equipe* in France, *La Gazzetta dello Sport* in Italy, *Marca* in Spain, and the now defunct *Sporting Life* in Britain, American magazines such as *Sports Illustrated* and the *Sporting News*, all-sports talk radio stations, and television networks such as Eurosport, ESPN and The Sports Network (TSN).

Sports teams are not always very accommodating to journalists: in the United States, while they allow reporters into locker rooms for interviews and some extra information, sports teams provide extensive information support, even if reporting it is unfavourable to them.

Elsewhere in the world, particularly in the coverage of soccer, the journalist's role is often barely tolerated by the clubs and players. For example, despite contractual media requirements in the English Premier League, prominent managers Sir Alex Ferguson (of Manchester United) and Harry Redknapp (first at Portsmouth, now at Tottenham) have refused to conduct post-match interviews with the BBC because of unfavourable coverage by the television channel's news department.

Sports journalists ought to be like reporters on other news beats, in that they must find the story, rather than simply relying on press releases and prepared statements from the sports team, coaching staff, or players. Sports journalists verify facts given to them by the athletes, teams, leagues, or organisations they are covering.

Access for sports journalists is usually easier for north American professional and intercollegiate sports such as football, ice hockey, basketball and baseball where the commercial relationship between media coverage and increased ticket, merchandise, or advertising sales, is better understood.

Socio-Political Importance

Major League Baseball gave print journalists a special role in its games: They were named official scorers and kept statistics that were considered part of the official record of the league. Active sportswriters were removed from this role in 1980. Although their statistical judgment calls could not affect the outcome of a game in progress, the awarding of errors and wins/saves were seen as powerful influences on pitching staff selections and play lists when coach decisions seemed unusual.

The removal of writers, who could benefit fiscally from sensational sports stories, was done to remove this perception of a conflict of interest, and to increase statistics volume, consistency, and accuracy. Sports stories occasionally transcend the games themselves and take on socio-political significance: Jackie Robinson breaking the color barrier in baseball is an example of this. Modern controversies regarding the hyper-compensation of top athletes, the use of anabolic steroids and other, banned performance-enhancing drugs, and the cost to local and national governments to build sports venues and related infrastructure, especially for Olympic Games, also demonstrate how sports intrudes on to the news pages. Sportswriters regularly face more deadline pressure than other reporters because sporting events tend to occur late in the day and closer to the deadlines many organisations must observe.

Yet they are expected to use the same tools as news journalists, and to uphold the same professional and ethical standards. They must take care not to show bias for any team. Many of the most talented and respected print journalists have been sportswriters.

The tradition of sports reporting attracting some of the finest writers in journalism can be traced to the coverage of sport in Victorian England, where several modern sports - such as association football, cricket, athletics and rugby - were first organised and codified into something resembling what we would recognize today.

Cricket, somewhat like baseball in the United States, possibly because of its esteemed place in society, has regularly attracted the most elegant of writers. The *Manchester*

Guardian, in the first half of the 20th Century, employed Neville Cardus as its cricket correspondent as well as its music critic. Cardus was later knighted for his services to journalism. One of his successors, John Arlott, who became a worldwide favourite because of his radio commentaries on the BBC, and was also known for his poetry.

The first London Olympic Games in 1908 attracted such widespread public interest that many newspapers assigned their very best-known writers to the event. The *Daily Mail* even had Sir Arthur Conan Doyle at the White City Stadium to cover the finish of the first ever 26-mile, 385-yard Marathon.

Such was the drama of that race, in which Dorando Pietri collapsed within sight of the finishing line when leading, that Conan Doyle led a public subscription campaign to see the gallant Italian, having been denied the gold medal through his disqualification, awarded a special silver cup, which was presented by Queen Alexandra. And the public imagination was so well caught by the event that annual races in Boston, Ma, and London, and at future Olympics, were henceforward staged over exactly the same, 26-mile, 385-yard distance, the official length of the event worldwide to this day.

The London race, called the Polytechnic Marathon and originally staged over the 1908 Olympic route from outside the royal residence at Windsor Castle to White City, was first sponsored by the *Sporting Life*, which in those Edwardian times was a daily newspaper which sought to cover all sporting events, rather than just a betting paper for horse racing and greyhounds that it became in the years after the Second World War.

In France, *L'Auto*, the predecessor of *L'Equipe*, had

already played an equally influential part in the sporting fabric of society when it announced in 1903 that it would stage an annual bicycle race around the country. The Tour de France was born, and sports journalism's role in its foundation is still reflected today in the leading rider wearing a yellow jersey - the color of the paper on which *L'Auto* was published (in Italy, the Giro d'Italia established a similar tradition, with the leading rider wearing a jersey the same pink color as the sponsoring newspaper, *La Gazzetta*).

After the World War II, the sports sections of British national daily and Sunday newspapers continued to expand, to the point where many papers now have separate standalone sports sections; some Sunday tabloids even have sections, additional to the sports pages, devoted solely to the previous day's football reports. In some respects, this has replaced the earlier practice of many regional newspapers which - until overtaken by the pace of modern electronic media - would produce special results editions rushed out on Saturday evenings. Some newspapers, such as the *The Sunday Times*, with 1924 Olympic 100 m champion Harold Abrahams, or the London *Evening News* using former England cricket captain Sir Leonard Hutton, began to adopt the policy of hiring former sports stars to pen columns, which were often ghost written.

Some such ghosted columns, however, did little to further the reputation of sports journalism, which is increasingly becoming the subject of academic scrutiny of its standards. Sportswriting in Britain has attracted some of the finest journalistic talents. The *Daily Mirror*'s Peter Wilson, Hugh McIlvanney, first at *The Observer* and lately at the *Sunday Times*, Ian Wooldridge of the *Daily Mail* and soccer writer Brian Glanville, best known at the *Sunday Times*, became household names in the late 20th Century through their trenchant reporting of often earth-shattering events that have transcended the back pages and been reported on the front pages: the Massacre at the Munich Olympics in 1972; Muhammad Ali's fight career, including his 1974 title bout against George Foreman; the Heysel Stadium disaster; and the career highs and lows of the likes of George Best and Lester Piggott and other high profile stars.

McIlvanney and Wooldridge, who died in March 2007, aged 75, both enjoyed careers that saw them frequently work in television. During his career, Wooldridge became so famous that, like the sports stars he reported upon, he hired the services of IMG, the agency founded by the American businessman, Mark McCormack, to manage his affairs. And Glanville wrote several books, including novels, as well as scripting the memorable official film to the 1966 World Cup staged in England.

Specialist Sports Agencies

The 1950s and 1960s saw a rapid growth in sports coverage, both in print and on broadcast media. It also saw the development of specialist sports news and photographic agencies. For example, photographer Tony Duffy founded the picture agency AllSport in south London shortly after the 1964 Tokyo Olympics, and, through some outstanding photography (such as Duffy's iconic image of the American long jumper Bob Beamon flying through the air towards his world record at the 1968 Mexico City Olympics) and the astute marketing of its images, saw the business grow into a multi-million pound, worldwide concern that ultimately would be bought and re-named Getty Images.

Sports Books

Increasingly, sports journalists have turned to long-form writing, producing popular books on a range of sporting topics, including biographies, history and investigations.

In London, through the 1980s and 1990s, one shop on Charing Cross Road - the area known for its book shops - was entirely devoted to sport, although the growth of online book sales through websites such as Amazon eventually led to the closure of Sports Books.

This was not before, though, the establishment, through sponsorship from William Hill, the bookmakers, of an annual prize for the sports book of the year. This was first held in 1989, when Dan Topolski's book about one of the most controversial University Boat Races was declared the winner.

The status of the awards, and of sports books generally, were enhanced greatly in 1992 when Nick Hornby's first novel, *Fever Pitch*, took first prize. Both *Fever Pitch* and *True Blue: The Oxford Boat Race Mutiny* have subsequently been adapted into feature-length motion pictures. Only one author, Donald McRae, in 1996 and 2002, has won the William Hill award more than once.

Unsurprisingly, given cricket writers' often literary aspirations and the appetite for books on cricket, the summer game has four times been the subject of the prize-winning book, the same number as football.

The award has not been without controversy in recent years. In 2000, the award went for the first time to a "ghosted" book, Lance Armstrong's *It's Not About the Bike*. At the time, some also observed the irony of the award going to the American Tour de France winner, when, in 1990, Paul Kimmage's stern critique of doping in cycling, *Rough Ride*, had been declared the winner.

The judges - the same panel is used each year - were

also criticised in 2006 when they chose Geoffrey Ward's *Unforgivable Blackness*, because it had been first published in 2004.

The 2007 winner of the award, announced at a ceremony staged at Waterstones, Piccadilly, on November 27, was *Provided You Don't Kiss Me*, the account of local newspaper reporter Duncan Hamilton working with the controversial Nottingham Forest manager, Brian Clough.

Winners of the William Hill Sports Book of the Year

- 2008: *Coming Back To Me*, Marcus Trescothick (with Peter Hayter)
- 2007: *Provided You Don't Kiss Me*, Duncan Hamilton
- 2006: *Unforgivable Blackness*, Geoffrey Ward
- 2005: *My Father and other Working Football Class Heroes*, Gary Imlach
- 2004: *Basil D'Oliveira*, Peter Oborne
- 2003: *Broken Dreams*, Tom Bower
- 2002: *In Black & White*, Donald McRae
- 2001: *Seabiscuit - The True Story Of 3 Men & A Race Horse*, Laura Hillenbrand
- 2000: *It's Not About the Bike - My Journey Back to Life*, Lance Armstrong
- 1999: *A Social History of English Cricket*, Derek Birley
- 1998: *Angry White Pyjamas*, Robert Twigger
- 1997: *A Lot Of Hard Yakka*, Simon Hughes
- 1996: *Dark Trade*, Donald McRae
- 1995: *A Good Walk Spoiled*, John Feinstein

- 1994: *Football Against The Enemy*, Simon Kuper
- 1993: *Endless Winter*, Stephen Jones
- 1992: *Fever Pitch*, Nick Hornby
- 1991: *Muhammad Ali: His Life and Times*, Thomas Hauser
- 1990: *Rough Ride*, Paul Kimmage
- 1989: *True Blue*, Dan Topolski

Investigative Journalism and Sport

Since the 1990s, the growing importance of sport, its impact as a global business and the huge amounts of money involved from sponsorship and in the staging of the Olympic Games and football World Cups, has also attracted the attention of well-known investigative journalists. The sensitive nature of the relationships between sports journalists and the subjects of their reporting, as well as declining budgets experienced by most Fleet Street newspapers, has meant that such long-term projects have often emanated from television documentary makers.

Tom Bower, with his 2003 sports book of the year *Broken Dreams*, which analysed British football, followed in the tradition established a decade earlier by Andrew Jennings and Vyv Simson with their controversial investigation of corruption within the International Olympic Committee. Jennings and Simson's *The Lords of the Rings* in many ways predicted the scandals that were to emerge around the staging of the 2002 Winter Olympics in Salt Lake City; Jennings would follow-up with two further books on the Olympics and one on FIFA, the world football body. Likewise, award-winning writers Duncan Mackay, of *The Guardian*, and Steven Downes unravelled many scandals involving doping, fixed races and bribery in international athletics in their 1996 book, *Running Scared*, which offered an account of the threats by a senior track official that led to the suicide of their sports journalist colleague, Cliff Temple.

But the writing of such exposes - referred to as "spitting in the soup" by Paul Kimmage, the former Tour de France professional cyclist, who now writes for the *Sunday Times* - often requires the view of an outsider who is not compromised by the need of day-to-day dealings with sportsmen and officials, as required by "beat" correspondents.

The stakes can be high when upsetting sport's powers: when in 2007, the English FA opted to switch its multi-million pound contract for UK coverage rights of the FA Cup and England international matches from the BBC to rival broadcasters ITV, one of the reasons cited was that the BBC had been too critical of the performances of the England football team.

Sports Journalism Organisations

Most countries have their own national association of sports journalists. Many sports also have their own clubs and associations for specialist journalists. These organisations tend not to operate as trades unions, but do attempt to maintain the standard of press provision at sports venues, oversee fair accreditation procedures and to celebrate high standards of sports journalism.

In Britain, the Sports Journalists' Association was founded in 1948. It stages two prestigious awards events, an annual Sports Awards ceremony which recognises outstanding performances by British sportsmen and women during the previous year, and the British Sports Journalism Awards, the industry's "Oscars", sponsored by UK Sport and presented each March.

Originally founded as the Sports Writers' Association, following a merger with the Professional Sports Photographers' Association in 2002 the organisation changed its title to the more inclusive SJA.

Its President is the veteran broadcaster and columnist, Sir Michael Parkinson.

The SJA represents the British sports media on the British Olympic Association's press advisory committee and acts as a consultant to organizers of major events who need guidance on media requirements as well as seeking to represent its members' interests in a range of activities.

In March 2008, Martin Samuel, then the chief football correspondent of *The Times*, was named British Sportswriter of the Year, the first time any journalist had managed to win the award three years in succession.

At the same awards, Jeff Stelling, of Sky Sports, was named Sports Broadcaster of the Year for the third time, a prize determined by a ballot of SJA members.

The International Sports Press Association, AIPS, was founded in 1924 during the Olympic Games in Paris, at the headquarters of the Sporting Club de France, by Frantz Reichel, the press chief of the Paris Games, and the Belgian, Victor Boin.

The first statutes of AIPS mentioned these objectives:

- to enhance the cooperation between its member associations in defending sport and the professional interest of their members.
- to strengthen the friendship, solidarity and common interests between sports journalists of all countries.

- to assure the best possible working conditions for the members.

AIPS operates through a system of continental sub-associations and national associations, and liaises closely with some of the world's biggest sports federations, including the International Olympic Committee, FIFA, football's world governing body and the IAAF, the international track and field body.

Fanzines and Blogs

Through the 1970s and '80s, a rise in "citizen journalism" in Europe was witnessed in the rapid growth in popularity of soccer "fanzines" - cheaply printed magazines written by fans for fans that bypassed often stilted official club match programmes and traditional media. Many continue today and thrive.

Some authors have been adopted by their clubs - Jim Munro, once editor of the West Ham United fanzine *Fortune's Always Dreaming*, was hired by the club to write for its matchday magazine and is now sports editor of The Sun Online. Other titles, such as the irreverent monthly soccer magazine *When Saturday Comes*, have effectively gone mainstream.

The advent of the internet has seen much of this fan-generated energy directed into sports blogs. Ranging from team-centric blogs to those that cover the sports media itself, Deadspin.com, Pro Football Talk, AOL Fanhouse, the blogs in the Yardbarker Network, and others have garnered massive followings.

Blogging has also been taken up by sportsmen and women such as Curt Schilling, Paula Radcliffe, Greg Oden, Donovan McNabb, and Chris Cooley.

TRADE JOURNALISM

Trade journalism reports on the movements and developments of the business world by way of articles or analysis. It usually operates in a fast-paced environment to match its subject matter, which often results in trade journals being online, to capture the ever-changing nature of the business industry. Trade journalism also refers to industry-specific news, such as exclusive focus on commodities (e.g. oil, gas and metals) or sectors (finance, travel, food). Due to its business nature, trade journalism is often expected to process and interpret a substantial amount of market commentary.

REFERENCES

Baase, S. "A Gift of Fire". PrentBaase, S. "A Gift of Fire". Prentice Hall, 3nd edition, 2008.

Beuttler, Bill. "Whatever Happened to the New Journalism?". BillBeuttler.com. http://billbeuttler.com/work50.htm. Retrieved on 2007-09-09.

Bowman, S. and Willis, C. "We Media: How Audiences are Shaping the Future of News and Information." 2003, *The Media Center at the American Press Institute*.

Dvorkin, J. A. "Media Matters. Can Public Radio Journalism be Re-Invented?" January 27, 2005, *National Public Radio*.

Flew, Terry "New Media: An Introduction". Oxford University Press, Melbourne.

Glaser, M. "The New Voices: Hyperlocal Citizen Media Sites Want You (to Write)!" November 17, 2004, *Online Journalism Review*.

George, E. "Guest Writer Liz George of Baristanet Reviews Backfence.com Seven Months After Launch." November 30, 2005, *Pressthink*.

Grubisich, T. "Grassroots journalism: Actual content vs. shining ideal." October 6, 2005, *USC Annenberg, Online Journalism Review*.

Kovach, B. and Rosenstiel, T. 2006. The Elements of Journalism; What Newspeople Should Know and the Public Should Expect.

Little Bill Clinton, *The Christian Science Monitor*'s serial following a year in the life of a young Congolese refugee.

Lasica, J. D. "What is Participatory Journalism?" 2003-08-07, *Online Journalism Review*, August 7, 2003.

Maher, V. "Citizen Journalism is Dead." 2005, New Media Lab, School of Journalism & Media Studies, Rhodes University, South Africa.

Meyer, E. P. "Public Journalism and the Problem of Objectivity." 1995, Published on personal website.

Merritt, D. "News Media must regain vigor, courage." September 29, 2004, *PJNet Today*.

Papandrea, Mary-Rose. "Citizen Journalism and the Reporter's Privilege." *Boston College Law School (Minnesota Law Review, Vol. 91)*. 2007. Retrieved on January 7, 2007.

Paul Levinson. 1997. The Soft Edge: a Natural History and Future of the Information Revolution, Routledge, London and New York, p. 39.

Robert Taft, *Photography and the American scene: A social history, 1839–1889* (New York: Dover, 1964), 446; and W. Joseph Campbell, "1897: American journalism's exceptional year", *Journalism History* 29 (2004) (also here *et seq.*)

Rosen, Jay "The People Formerly Known as the Audience," PressThink, June 27, 2006.

The Poynter Institut, A school dedicated to teaching and inspiring journalists and media leaders.

Walker, L. "On Local Sites, Everyone's A Journalist, December 9, 2004, *Washington Post*, E1.

Wolfe, Tom (1987-12-18). "The bonfire of the vanities". *National Review*. http://www.findarticles.com/p/articles/mi_m1282/is_n24_v39/ai_6199633. Retrieved on 2007-09-09.

World Press Photo; Best of Photojournalism; Pictures of the Year; The Press Photographer's Year.

[*Courtesy:* Wikipedia]

4

Radio Jockey (RJ) and Disc Jockey (DJ)

Chronology

19th Century to 1920s

In 1857, Leon Scott invented the phonoautograph in France, the first device to record sound. In 1877, Charles Cros invented the phonograph in France (it was patented before Edison's invention but never built) and Thomas Alva Edison invented the phonograph cylinder, the first device to play back recorded sound, in the United States. In 1892, Emile Berliner began commercial production of his gramophone records, the first disc records to be offered to the public. In 1906, Reginald Fessenden transmitted the first audio radio broadcast in history also playing the first record, that of a contralto singing Handel's *Largo* from *Xerxes*. The world's first radio disc jockey was Ray Newby, of Stockton, California. In 1909, at 16 years of age, Newby began regularly playing records on a small spark transmitter while a student at Herrold College of Engineering and Wireless, located in San Jose, California, under the authority of radio pioneer Charles "Doc" Herrold.

> We used popular records at that time, mainly Caruso records, because they were very good and loud; we needed

> a boost... we started on an experimental basis and then, because this is novel, we stayed on schedule continually without leaving the air at any time from that time on except for a very short time during World War I, when the government required us to remove the antenna... Most of our programming was records, I'll admit, but of course we gave out news as we could obtain it...
>
> —*Ray Newby, I've Got a Secret (1965)*

By 1910, regular radio broadcasting had started to use "live" as well as prerecorded sound. In the early radio age, content typically included comedy, drama, news, music, and sports reporting. The on-air announcers and programmers would later be known as disc jockeys. In the 1920s, juke joints became popular as places for dancing and drinking to recorded jukebox music. In 1927, Christopher Stone became the first radio announcer and programmer in the United Kingdom, on the BBC radio station. In 1929, Thomas Edison ceased phonograph cylinder manufacture, ending the disc and cylinder rivalry.

1930s–1950s

In 1935, American commentator Walter Winchell coined the term "disc jockey" (the combination of "disc" (referring to the disc records) and "jockey" (which is an operator of a machine) as a description of radio announcer Martin Block, the first announcer to become a star. While his audience was awaiting developments in the Lindbergh kidnapping, Block played records and created the illusion that he was broadcasting from a ballroom, with the nation's top dance bands performing live. The show, which he called *Make Believe Ballroom*, was an instant hit. The term "disc jockey" appeared in print in *Variety* in 1941. In 1943, Jimmy Savile launched the world's first DJ dance party by playing jazz records in the upstairs function room of the Loyal Order of Ancient Shepherds in Otley, England. In 1947, he became the first DJ to use twin turntables for continuous play. Also in 1947, the Whiskey à Go-Go nightclub opened in Paris, France, considered to be the world's first discothèque, or disco (deriving its name from the French word meaning a nightclub where the featured entertainment is recorded music rather than an on-stage band). Discos began appearing across Europe and the United States. From the late 1940s to early 1950s, the introduction of television eroded the popularity of radio's early format, causing it to take on the general form it has today, with a strong focus on music, news, and sports. In the 1950s, American radio DJs would appear live at "sock hops" and "platter parties" and assume the role of a human jukebox. They would usually play 45-rpm records, featuring hit singles on one turntable while talking between songs. In some cases, a live drummer was hired to play beats between songs to maintain the dance floor.

In 1955, Bob Casey, a well-known "sock hop" DJ, introduced the first two-turntable system for alternating back and forth between records, creating a continuous playback of music. Throughout the 1950s, payola payments by record companies to DJs in return for airplay were an ongoing problem. Part of the fallout from the payola scandal was tighter control of the music by station management. The Top 40 format emerged, where popular songs are played repeatedly.

In the late 1950s, sound systems, a new form of public entertainment, were developed in the ghettos of Kingston, Jamaica. Promoters, who called themselves DJs, would throw large parties in the streets that centered on the disc jockey, called the "selector," who played dance music from large, loud PA systems and bantered over the music with a boastful, rhythmic chanting style called "toasting." These parties quickly became profitable for the promoters, who would sell admission, food, and alcohol, leading to fierce competition between DJs for the biggest sound systems and newest records.

1960s and 1970s

In the mid-1960s, nightclubs and discotheques continued to grow in Europe and the United States. Specialized DJ equipment, such as Rudy Bozak's classic CMA-10-2DL mixer, began to appear on the market. In 1969, American club DJ Francis Grasso popularized beatmatching at New York's Sanctuary nightclub. Beatmatching is the technique of creating seamless transitions between records with *matching beats*, or tempos. Grasso also developed slip-cuing, the technique of holding a record still while the turntable is revolving underneath, releasing it at the desired moment to create a sudden transition from the previous record.

By 1968, the number of dance clubs started to decline; most American clubs either closed or were transformed into clubs featuring live bands. Neighborhood block parties that were modelled after Jamaican sound systems gained popularity in Europe and in the boroughs of New York City. During the early 1970s, the economic downturn led most of the dance clubs to become underground gay discos.

In 1973, Jamaican-born DJ Kool Herc, widely regarded as the "godfather of hip-hop culture," performed at block parties in his Bronx neighborhood and developed a technique of mixing back and forth between two identical records to extend the rhythmic instrumental segment, or *break*. Turntablism, the art of using turntables not only to play music but to manipulate sound and create original music, began to develop. In 1974, Technics released the first SL-

1200 turntable, which evolved into the SL-1200 MK2 in 1979—which, as of the mid-2000s, remains the industry standard for deejaying.

In 1974, German electronic music band Kraftwerk released the 22-minute song "Autobahn," which takes up the entire first side of that LP. Years later, Kraftwerk would become a significant influence on hip-hop artists such as Afrika Bambaataa and house music pioneer Frankie Knuckles. During the mid-1970s, Hip-hop music and culture began to emerge, originating among urban African Americans and Latinos in New York City. The four main elements of hip-hop culture were MCing (rapping), DJing, graffiti, and breakdancing.

In the mid-1970s, the soul-funk blend of dance pop known as disco took off in the mainstream pop charts in the United States and Europe, causing discotheques to experience a rebirth. Unlike many late-1960s clubs, which featured live bands, discotheques used the DJ's selection and mixing of records as the entertainment. In 1975, record pools began, providing disc jockeys access to newer music from the industry in an efficient method.

In 1976, American DJ, editor, and producer Walter Gibbons remixed "Ten Percent" by Double Exposure, one of the earliest commercially released 123† singles (aka "maxi-single"). In 1977, hip-hop DJ Grand Wizard Theodore invented the scratching technique by accident. In 1979, the Sugar Hill Gang released "Rapper's Delight," the first hip-hop record to become a hit. It was also the first real breakthrough for sampling, as the bassline of Chic's "Good Times" laid the foundation for the song.

In 1977, Saratoga Springs, NY disc jockey Tom L.

Lewis introduced the Disco Bible (later renamed Disco Beats), which published hit disco songs listed by beats per minute (tempo), as well as by either artist or song title. Billboard ran an article on the new publication, and it went national relatively quickly. The list made it easier for beginning DJs to learn how to create seamless transitions between songs without dancers having to change their rhythm on the dance floor.

1980s

In 1981, the cable television network MTV was launched, originally devoted to music videos, especially popular rock music. The term "video jockey," or VJ, was used to describe the fresh-faced youth who introduced the music videos. In 1982, the demise of disco in the mainstream by the summer of 1982 forced many nightclubs to either close or change entertainment styles, such as by providing MTV-style video dancing or live bands. Released in 1982, the song "Planet Rock" by DJ Afrika Bambaataa was the first hip-hop song to feature synthesizers. The song melded electronic hip-hop beats with the melody from Kraftwerk's "Trans-Europe Express." In 1982, the Compact Disc reached the public market in Asia, and early the following year in other markets. This event is often seen as the "Big Bang" of the digital audio revolution.

In the early 1980s, NYC disco DJ Larry Levan, known for his eclectic mixes, gained a cult following, and the Paradise Garage, the nightclub at which he spun, became the prototype for the modern dance club where the music and the DJ were showcased. Around the same time, the disco-influenced electronic style of dance music called house music emerged in Chicago. The name was derived from the Warehouse Club in Chicago, where resident DJ Frankie Knuckles mixed old disco classics and Eurosynth pop. House music is essentially disco music with electronic drum machine beats. The common element of most house music is a 4/4 beat generated by a drum machine or other electronic means (such as a sampler), together with a solid (usually also electronically generated) synth bassline. In 1983, Jesse Saunders released what some consider the first house music track, "On & On." The mid-1980s also saw the emergence of New York Garage, a house music hybrid that was inspired by Levan's style and sometimes eschewed the accentuated high-hats of the Chicago house sound.

During the mid-1980s, techno music emerged from the Detroit club scene. Being geographically located between Chicago and New York, Detroit techno artists combined elements of Chicago house and New York garage along with European imports. Techno distanced itself from disco's roots by becoming almost purely electronic with synthesized beats. In 1985, the Winter Music Conference started in Fort Lauderdale Florida and became the premier electronic music conference for dance music disc jockeys. In 1985, TRAX Dance Music Guide was launched by American Record Pool in Beverly Hills. It was the first national DJ-published music magazine, created on the Macintosh computer using extensive music market research and early desktop publishing tools. In 1986, "Walk This Way," a rap/rock collaboration by Run DMC and Aerosmith, became the first hip-hop song to reach the Top 10 on the Billboard Hot 100. This song was the first exposure of hip-hop music, as well as the concept of the disc jockey as band member and artist, to many mainstream audiences. In 1988, *DJ Times* magazine was first published. It was the first US-based magazine specifically geared toward the professional mobile and club DJ. Starting in the mid-1980s, the wedding and banquet business changed dramatically with the introduction of DJ music, replacing the bands that had been the norm.

Bandleaders, like Jerry Perell and others, started DJ companies, such as NY Rhythm DJ Entertainers. Using their knowledge of audience participation, MC charisma, and "crowd-pleasing" repertory selection, the wedding music industry became almost all DJ while combining the class and elegance of the traditional band presentation. New DJs as well as bandleaders with years of experience and professionalism transformed the entire industry. Now, everyone loves a good banquet DJ. The latest trend is to combine real musicians with the DJ music for a more personal and artistic approach.

1990s-2000s

During the early 1990s, the rave scene built on the acid house scene. Some DJs, wanting to be the only source for hearing certain tunes, used "white labels" — records with no info printed on them — in an effort to prevent other trainspotters from learning what they were spinning. The rave scene changed dance music, the image of DJs, and the nature of promoting. The innovative marketing surrounding the rave scene created the first superstar DJs who established marketable "brands" around their names and sound. Some of these celebrity DJs toured around the world and were able to branch out into other music-related activities.

During the early 1990s, the Compact Disc surpassed the gramophone record in popularity, but gramophone records continued to be made (although in very limited quantities) into the 21st century — particularly for club DJs and for local acts recording on small regional labels. During the mid-1990s, trance music, having run rampant in the German underground for several years, emerged as a major force in dance music throughout Europe and the UK. It became one of the world's most dominant forms dance music by the end of the 1990s, thanks to a trend away from its repetitive, hypnotic roots, and towards commercialized song structure.

In 1991, *Mobile Beat* magazine, geared specifically toward mobile DJs, began publishing. In 1992, MPEG which stands for the Moving Picture Experts Group, released The MPEG-1 standard, designed to produce reasonable sound at low bit rates. The lossy compression scheme MPEG-1 Layer-3, popularly known as MP3, later revolutionized the digital music domain. In 1993, the first internet "radio station", Internet Talk Radio, was developed by Carl Malamud. Because the audio was relayed over the internet, it was possible to access internet radio stations from anywhere in the world. This made it a popular service for both amateur and professional disc jockeys operating from a personal computer.

In 1995, the first full-time, internet-only radio station, Radio HK, began broadcasting the music of independent bands. In 1996, Mobile Beat had its first national mobile DJ convention in Las Vegas. During the late 1990s, nu metal bands, such as Korn, Limp Bizkit, and Linkin Park, reached the height of their popularity. This new subgenre of alternative rock bore some influence from hip-hop because rhythmic innovation and syncopation are primary, often featuring DJs as band members. As well, during the late 1990s, various DJ and VJ software programmes were developed, allowing personal computer users to deejay or veejay using his or her personal music or video files.

In 1998, the first MP3 digital audio player was released, the Eiger Labs MPMan F10. Final Scratch debuted at the BE Developer Conference, marking the first digital DJ system to allow DJs control of MP3 files through special time coded vinyl records or CDs. While it would take sometime for this novel concept to catch on with the "die hard Vinyl DJs", This would soon become the first step in the new Digital DJ revolution. Manufacturers joined with computer DJing pioneers to offer professional endorsements, the first being Professor Jam, who went on to develop the industry's first dedicated computer DJ convention and learning program, the "CPS (Computerized Performance System) DJ Summit", to help spread the word about the advantages of this emerging technology. In 1999, Shawn Fanning released Napster, the first of the massively popular peer-to-peer file sharing systems. During this period, the AVLA (Audio Video Licensing Agency) of Canada announced an MP3 DJing license, administered by the Canadian Recording Industry Association. This meant that DJs could apply for a license giving them the right to "burn" their own compilation CDs of "usable tracks", instead of having to cart their whole CD collections around to their gigs.

By the 2000s, new technologies such as voice tracking, allowed single DJs to send announcements across many stations. Commercial radio DJs were increasingly limited in their freedom to select which songs to play. Some music aficionados sought freeform stations that put the DJs back in control, or chose instead to listen to satellite radio services or portable music players. College radio stations and other public radio outlets continued to be the most common places for freeform play lists in the U.S.

In 2001, Apple Computer's iPod was introduced and quickly became the highest selling brand of portable digital mp3 audio player. The convenience and popularity of the iPod spawned a new type of DJ, the "MP3J". First appearing in certain East London clubs, and spreading to other music scenes, including New York City, this new DJ scene allowed the average music fan to bring two iPods to an "iPod

Night", plug in to the mixer, and programme a play list without the skill and equipment demanded by a more traditional DJ setup, and without needing to bring a heavy case of CDs. In 2004 Rane introduced its own version of the digital vinyl DJ system Serato Scratch Live making improvements in overall system stability and more closely emulating the feel of true vinyl. They brought out a hardware mixer version in 2006. Soon afterward, many nightclub deejays that had remained true vinyl record aficionados began the transition to becoming digital vinyl users. In 2006, the concept of DJ had its 100-year anniversary. In the late 2000s, topless female DJs have appeared in special nightclubs, primarily in Finland and Russia.

RADIO JOCKEY (RJ)

A radio jockey or RJ is a person who hosts a radio talk show, where he/she selects the music to be played by interacting with the audience via telephone. Lately, the term started to be associated with radio show hosts who interact online with viewers, with or without playing a song. Etymologically, the term roots from disc jockey, a term used to describe a person who plays music in discos. However it is still uncertain when it first became popular. Its origin clearly shows a regional bias as although quite generic in description, it is used specifically in India. This confirms its Indian origin.

Today, Radio Jockeying is considered to be a 'hot' profession and these voices have become so famous, that they have become household names like Ameen Sayani, Shamshir, Karan, Nitin, Dev, Rajeev Tyagi, Hardeep Chandpuri etc. Today they simply rule the 'air waves'. One of the most respected names in India in the field of Radio Jockey training is the Academy of Broadcasting which was set up in the year 2003, by internationally renowned Radio Jockey Hardeep Singh Chandpuri, the person responsible for revolutionising the radio scene in north India. The medium of radio, which was once considered to be the synonym of boredom for the youngsters, achieved brand new heights with his fresh style of presentation and today it is his name that is associated with the complete 'makeover' of the radio scene in the northern region besides this he is also well-known for training and grooming the Radio Jockeys of tomorrow and today.

There are numerous media houses that have branched into the radio scene. Because of the high licensing fees and limited wave bands being made available only big, corporate houses can be found in the scene with almost no small companies and definitely no individuals in sharp contrast to Western radio where there are many small-time players. This is why there is also a great difference between being in radio abroad as compared to India. Because there are relatively fewer radio stations and RJs, Radio Jockeys tend to have a fan-following; where people will listen to their show to the exclusion of all others and RJs at times, even successfully endorse brands or products in their shows. Due to this scenario, Radio Jockeys (RJs) have a very high popularity and even become celebrities in some cases.

Some of the better known RJs in various leading cities in India include:

1. RJ Mantra- Winner of the RAPA Award 2008
2. RJ Denny- Radio Mirchi Nagpur-His evening prime-time show is a huge hit and he's a celebrity in town.
3. RJ Aniruddh- who was Pune's morning RJ then went on abroad.

4. RJ Nitin- popularly known as Ulta Pulta Nitin- Red FM

Basically, RJs may start out on fixed salaries but they pay-packages can skyrocket after a few years in the business. Many go on to become Voice-over artistes and lend their voices to commercials, dubbed movies and even animated shows. Some RJs tend to go to other countries and host what are called "desi shows" i.e. shows with Indian influences. A radio jockey or RJ is a person who hosts a radio talk show, where he/she selects the music to be played by interacting with the audience via telephone. Lately, the term started to be associated with radio show hosts who interact online with viewers, with or without playing a song. Today, Radio Jockeying is considered to be a 'hot' profession and these voices have become so famous, that they have become household names like RJ SUNY Ameen Sayani, Shamshir, Karan, Nitin, Dev, Rajeev Tyagi, Hardeep Chandpuri etc. Today they simply rule the 'air waves'. One of the most respected names in India in the field of Radio Jockey training is the Academy of Broadcasting which was set-up in the year 2003, by internationally renowned Radio Jockey Hardeep Singh Chandpuri, the person responsible for revolutionising the radio scene in north India.

The medium of radio, which was once considered to be the synonym of boredom for the youngsters, achieved brand new heights with his fresh style of presentation and today it is his name that is associated with the complete 'makeover' of the radio scene in the northern region besides this he is also well-known for training and grooming the Radio Jockeys of tomorrow and today.

There are numerous media houses that have branched into the radio scene. Because of the high licensing fees and limited wave bands being made available only big, corporate houses can be found in the scene with almost no small companies and definitely no individuals in sharp contrast to Western radio where there are many small-time players.

DISC JOCKEY

A disc jockey or disk jockey (also known as DJ or deejay) is a person who selects and plays recorded music for an audience. Originally, disk referred to phonograph records, while disc refers to the Compact Disc, and has become the more common spelling.

A video jockey or VJ serves the same function for music videos. There are several types of disc jockeys. Radio DJs introduce and play music that is broadcast on AM, FM, shortwave, digital, or internet radio stations. Club DJs select and play music in bars, nightclubs, discothèques, at raves, or even in a stadium. Hip-hop disc jockeys select and play music using multiple turntables, often to backup one or more MCs.

In reggae, the disc jockey (deejay) is a vocalist who raps, "toasts", or chats over pre-recorded rhythm tracks while the individual choosing and playing them is referred to as a selector. Mobile disc jockeys travel with portable sound systems and work at a variety of events.

Equipment and Techniques

DJ equipment may consist of:

- Sound recordings in a DJ's preferred medium (e.g., vinyl records, Compact Discs, computer media files, etc.);
- A combination of two devices (or sometimes one, if playback is digital) to play sound recordings, for

alternating back and forth to create a continuous playback of music (e.g., record players, Compact Disc players, computer media players such as an MP3 player, etc.);

- A sound system for amplification or broadcasting of the recordings (e.g., portable audio system, PA system) or a radio broadcasting system;
- A DJ mixer, which is an electronic (usually 2- or 4-channel) audio mixer with a crossfader used to smoothly go from one song to another, using two or more playback devices;
- Headphones, used to listen to one recording while the other recording is being played to the audience; and
- Optionally, a microphone, so that the DJ can introduce songs and speak to the audience.

Other equipment could or can be added to the basic DJ setup (above), providing unique sound manipulations. Such devices include, but are not limited to:

- Electronic effects units (delay, reverb, octave, equalizer, chorus, etc.). Some club DJs use a sub-harmonic synthesizer effect which either doubles low frequencies with energy added an octave lower or synthesizes harmonics such that the impression of a very low bass sound is added to the mix.
- A computerised performance system, which can be used with vinyl emulation software to manipulate digital files on the computer in real time.
- Multi-stylus headshells, which allow a DJ to play different grooves of the same record at the same time.

- Special DJ digital controller hardware can manipulate digital files on a PC or laptop;
- Samplers, sequencers, electronic musical keyboards (synthesizers), or drum machines.

Several techniques are used by DJs as a means to better mix and blend recorded music. These techniques primarily include the cuing, equalization, and audio mixing of two or more sound sources. The complexity and frequency of special techniques depends largely on the setting in which a DJ is working. Radio DJs are less likely to focus on music-mixing procedures than club DJs, who rely on a smooth transition between songs using a range of techniques.

Club DJ turntable techniques include beatmatching, phrasing, and slip-cueing to preserve energy on a dancefloor. Turntablism embodies the art of cutting, beat juggling, scratching, needle drops, phase shifting, back spinning, and more to perform the transitions and overdubs of samples in a more creative manner (although turntablism is often considered a use of the turntable as a musical instrument rather than a tool for blending recorded music). Professional DJs may use harmonic mixing to choose songs that are in compatible musical keys.

Kinds of DJ

The role of selecting and playing recorded music for an intended audience is the same for every disc jockey. The selected music, the audience, the setting, the preferred medium, and the level of sophistication of sound manipulation are factors that differentiate the various DJ types.

Radio Disc Jockeys

A radio disc jockey plays music that is broadcast across radio waves—AM and FM bands, or worldwide on shortwave radio stations. Radio DJs are often notable for their personalities. Famous American radio disc jockeys such as Alan Freed, Scott Muni, Casey Kasem, Dick Biondi, Wolfman Jack, and Dr. Demento built their audiences using a combination of the nature of the songs they selected and strong on-air personalities. A modern-day commercial radio disc jockey will typically rely on his or her on-air character alone, as the station's playlist has been predetermined by a programme director or music director. Radio disc jockeys appear in a wide range of broadcast formats, from top 40 or contemporary hit radio (CHR) to oldies and other formats that are defined by the type of songs played. Formats are defined by the type of originating station, with public radio, college radio, and pirate radio as examples. Some national governments operate official radio stations for a global audience, such as Voice of America (hosted by the United States) and Voice of Russia (organized by the Russian government).

These stations may include programmes by disc jockeys; The Clash frontman Joe Strummer played selections from his musical library for the UK's BBC World Service in the 1990s. Large military units sometimes broadcast their own radio programmes to their troops, inserting news, weather reports, and advice between popular songs.

Reggae Deejays

In reggae music (specifically dancehall), the deejay is traditionally a vocalist who raps, toasts, or chats to a "riddim." The term "selector" is reserved for the person who just selects the record and plays it over the sound system.

Club Disc Jockeys

Using several turntables, CD players, or a hard-drive source, a club disc jockey selects and plays music in a club setting. The setting can range anywhere from a neighborhood party or a small nightclub to a discotheque, a rave, or even a stadium. The main focus of club DJs is on the music they play and how they mix tracks in and out, sometimes just to add a bit of energy to a track. They build their sets by choosing tracks to control the energy level of the crowd and use beatmixing and beatmatching techniques for seamless transitions between tracks. For more information, see List of club DJs.

Hip-hop Disc Jockeys

A hip-hop disc jockey is a DJ that selects and plays music as a hip-hop artist and/or performer, often backing up one or more MCs.

Mobile Disc Jockeys

Mobile disc jockeys are an extension of the original radio disc jockeys. They travel with or go on tour with mobile sound systems and play from an extensive collection of recorded content for a specific audience. Today, mobile DJs need a large selection of music, professional-grade equipment, good organizational skills, vocal talent as an MC, mixing skills, quality lighting, insurance for liability, and on-site backup equipment. In the 2000s, the role of the mobile DJ has expanded. Many mobile DJs have assumed additional responsibilities to ensure an event's success. These responsibilities include the roles of MC, event organizer and coordinator, lighting director, and/or sound engineer.

In the past, Mobile DJs utilized vinyl records or cassettes. During the disco era of the 1970s, demand for mobile DJs (called "mobile discos" in the UK) soared, and top disc jockeys travelled with hundreds of vinyl records and cassette tapes. In the 1990s, Compact Discs became the standard. Mobile disc jockey trade publications such as *DJ Times* magazine and *Mobile Beat* were founded in this era. Mobile DJs have formed professional associations such as the Canadian Disc Jockey Association (CDJA), the Canadian Online Disc Jockey Association (CODJA), the American Disc Jockey Association (ADJA), and the National Association of Mobile Entertainers. In the UK, associations include the National Association of Disc Jockeys (NADJ) and the South Eastern Discotheque Association (SEDA). Today, many mobile DJs rely heavily on laptop computers and MP3s for sequencing and mixing. This technology allows DJs to do mixing prior to an event and also lightens the load by reducing the number of CDs that a DJ must carry.

How to Become a Radio Jockey

Radio Jockey (RJ) has been with us for almost a century, but since the advent of FM channels the Radio Announcer suddenly being referred as Radio Jockey or RJ. These days a RJ not only plays a part of the navigator but his/her main aim is to entertain the listeners and simultaneously provides regular online information. Every successful RJ has its own style of communicating. A sweet, mid to heavy voice is considered suitable for broadcasting but moreover it's your own aptitude, your overall confidence, your personality to deliver all of it through your voice. Although Radio Jockeys are required for all channels of Radio, but a Radio Jockey is usually related to FM. But why FM?. FM channel broadcasts in stereo and has very good sound quality as compared to other short, medium wave channels.

FM channels are relatively new medium and has gone through lot of changes since its formation. The style, expression, delivery, and content too have developed. FM Radio is a fast progressing industry with more and more channels opening up in every city of the world. First of all, an RJ does not have a regular 9 to 5 job. He can be called to host or anchor a show anytime of the day or night. An RJ has to be very open to himself. Whatever may be your emotions an RJ is always happy. He should be culturally active. He/She should know his/her city well, the culture and be aware of main events taking place. You should know of the language or further some dialects of other languages also, to punch in whenever necessary. Since Radio cannot survive without Movies, Songs or Bollywood in terms of India, so awareness about them is considered a necessity. An RJ should also be able to write scripts for a show. One thing more if you have written your script yourself, you know of the subject matter and can change or manipulate at your own will.

An RJ has also to anchor live shows. If speaking is your passion, talking to people comes naturally to you, fun never ends. Your every word is Live. You react to every song or item played. Everything is spontaneous but very relevant and entertaining. In short you may have the following qualities—

(i) You enjoy talking to people and have a desire to be aware.

(ii) You must be original and should have your own style.

(iii) Your other voice performance or qualities like mimicry, local dialects and comedy or humor items helps to carry on the show.

(iv) You should know how to provide variations and modulation in your voice. You should be fluent but not monotonous as this may create boredom in your audience monotone is a surefire way of losing your audience.

Modulate your voice well and your fan following will increase and open the way to other assignments. If you can sound different on your show, people will enjoy listening to you. Humans have a tendency to make mistake, if somehow a mistake has been made, either admit it or cover it up diplomatically. This may come up with experience or better listen to experienced RJs how they tackle these issues. Their professionalism, their relationship with listeners, the flow they are speaking, their interactiveness and so on. Also note how they interact live with listeners, how do they tackle some awkward queries or comments from callers. You should be ready to face that and cover up in your style quickly by changing the topic or by taking a break or playing a song.

Mostly the telephone callers are briefed before for a minute or so before they come on live, this gets you an idea of the caller. Another thing an RJ is familiarity with the sound equipment and computers. An RJ has to deal with sound mixers, faders, CD players, Call equipment, Computer for his songs and Ads database and microphones & headphones. An RJ has to be with them in his studio, so one has to be computer savvy or have a desire to learn more on that. He should be able to know, if a goof up happens or should switch over to alternate equipment quickly. Never the less there are technical support to help you.

No. Anchoring or Radio Jockeying depends on how you deliver, your originality, and the punch in your content, your style, your personality, how you present your programme and further how you connect with your audience. An RJ should have good communication powers and language skills. Never the less, RJ courses do help to develop your confidence or bring out your personality or inbuilt caliber in hiding but are not a necessity Many of the RJ's today have never gone through any course and have a good name today. RJ hunts or talent search are often conducted by FM channels to bring out original unique talent. There is a lot of scope for quick growth. All you need is talent, confidence and perseverance. As a radio jockey, besides getting contractual good money you earn by doing Ad commercials. As you get famous and your voice is recognized, other Radio Channels tend to attract you with better package. Alternatively RJs are also busy with doing voice-overs for ad films and movies. When they are being connected to their audience RJs also can anchor or compare TV shows or live shows / events.

Radio Jockey Education in India

It is pertinent to note that popularity of radio is suffering badly because of internet and television, but FM radio on the private channels gives new life to the radio. Radio jockey is very challenging, promising, and exciting option for those having favour of music. In this occupation, someone can be identified by their voice. The job of Radio Jockeys (RJ) is to anchor music related programmes on the radio. RJ entertains audience by playing songs and conveying messages in very effective and sophisticated way. They play requests from guests, listeners, arrange/ manage contests and gives information related to music, traffic or weather. Presence of mind and hard work is necessary for this occupation. Youngsters are mostly recommended for this post because they have new ideas and concepts regarding the shows. Each RJ has the friendly, warm, dynamic, and spontaneous and must have good communication. Every RJ has their own style to communicate with audience.

RJ should be diplomatic because they have to speak

with different types of people ond on different subjects. They must keep down-to-earth nature and good attitude so that listeners contentedly calls and speaks without any botheration.

Institutions

In fact formal training is not necessary for making the radio jockey.

Following are the premier institutions for imparting training to RJ in India:

- Xavier Institute of Communications, Mumbai
- Academy of Radio Management, Delhi
- Take One Academy of Broadcasting, Chandigarh

Placements and Prospects

Radio Jockey is having diversifying nature depends on the subject of the programmes. Their job is not regular. They may be called at any time for hosting or anchoring any show. The job of RJ includes writing scripts for show, presenting show, and select proper music suitable to that show. RJ becomes successful depending on shows presented by him and also depends on the listeners of the show. The speech should original, effective and interesting to the listeners. Radio jockey should write a script for the programme and should have knowledge of old and latest movie and the songs. He must be familiar with the computers and sound equipments.

5

Media Literacy and Training

As of now Media education is developing in Great Britain, Australia, South Africa, Canada, the United States, with a growing interest in the Netherlands, Italy, Greece, Austria, Switzerland, India, Russia and among many other nations. Media literacy is the process of accessing, analyzing, evaluating and creating messages in a wide variety of media modes, genres and forms. It uses an inquiry-based instructional model that encourages people to ask questions about what they watch, see and read. Media literacy education is one means of developing media literacy.

It provides tools to help people critically analyze messages to detect propaganda, censorship, and bias in news and public affairs programming (and the reasons for such), and to understand how structural features — such as media ownership, or its funding model — affect the information presented. Media literacy aims to enable people to be skillful creators and producers of media messages, both to facilitate an understanding as to the strengths and limitations of each medium, as well as to create independent media. Media literacy is an expanded conceptualisation of literacy.

By transforming the process of media consumption into an active and critical process, people gain greater awareness of the potential for misrepresentation and manipulation (especially through commercials and public relations techniques), and understand the role of mass media and participatory media in constructing views of reality. Media literacy was originally conceived as an educational tool to protect people from what many perceived to be mass media's ill effects. The earliest country known to use this inoculative paradigm was Great Britain in the 1930s. In the 1960s, there was a paradigm shift in the field of media literacy to emphasize working within popular culture rather than trying to convince people that popular culture was primarily destructive. This was known as the popular arts paradigm.

In the 1980s, there came a recognition that the ideological power of the media was tied to the naturalisation of the image. Constructed messages were being passed off as natural ones. The focus of media literacy also shifted to the consumption of images and representations, also known as the representational paradigm. In the United Kingdom and Australia media literacy is often a stand alone credit course, as well as part of the English curricula. In Australia, media education was influenced by developments in Britain related to the inoculation, popular arts and demystification approaches. Key theorists who influenced Australian media education were Graeme Turner and John Hartley who helped develop Australian media and cultural studies.

During the 1980s and 1990s, Western Australians Robyn Quin and Barrie MacMahon wrote seminal text books such as *Real Images*, translating many complex media theories into classroom appropriate learning frameworks. Currently, in most Australian states, media is one of five strands of the Arts Key Learning Area and includes "essential learnings" or "outcomes" listed for various stages of development. At the senior level (years 11 and 12), several states offer

Media Studies as an elective. For example, many Queensland schools offer Film, Television and New Media, while Victorian schools offer VCE Media.

Media education is supported by the teacher professional association Australian Teachers of Media (ATOM) which publishes a range of resources and the excellent Screen Education.

Notably, in European countries media education has seen many different forms. Media education was introduced into the Finnish elementary curriculum in 1970 and into high schools in 1977. But the media education we know today did not evolve in Finland until the 1990s. Media education has been compulsory in Sweden since 1980 and in Denmark since 1970. In both Nordic countries, media education evolved in the 1980s and 1990s as media education gradually moved away from moralizing attitudes towards an approach that is more searching and pupil-centred. In 1994, the Danish education bill gave recognition to media education but it is still not an integrated part of the school.

The focus in Denmark seems to be on information technology. France has taught film from the inception of the medium, but it has only been recently that conferences and media courses for teachers have been organised with the inclusion of media production. Germany saw theoretical publications on media literacy in the 1970s and 80s, with a growing interest for media education inside and outside the educational system in the 80s and 90s. In the Netherlands media literacy was placed in the agenda by the Dutch government in 2006 as an important subject for the Dutch society. In April, 2008, an official center has been created by the Dutch government.

This center is more a network organisation existing out

of different partners who have their own expertise with the subject of media education. The idea is that media education will become a part of the official curriculum. The history of Media Education in Russia goes back to the 1920s. The first attempts to instruct in media education (on the press and film materials, with the vigorous emphasis on the communist ideology) appeared in the 1920s but were stopped by Stalin's repressions. The end of the 1950s - the beginning of the 1960s was the time of the revival of media education in secondary schools, universities, after-school children centers (Moscow, Petersburg, Voronezh, Samara, Kurgan, Tver, Rostov, Taganrog, Novosibirsk, Ekaterinburg, etc.), the revival of media education seminars and conferences for the teachers. During the time when the intensive rethinking of media education approaches was on the upgrade in the Western hemisphere, in Russia of the 1970s–1980s media education was still developing within the aesthetic concept. Among the important achievements of 1970s-1990s one can recall the first official programmes of film and media education, published by Ministry of Education, increasing interest of Ph.D. to media education, experimental theoretic and practical work on media education by O.Baranov (Tver), S.Penzin (Voronezh), G.Polichko, U.Rabinovich (Kurgan), Y.Usov (Moscow), A.Fedorov (Taganrog), A.Sharikov (Moscow) and others. The important events in media education development in Russia are the registration of the new specialisation (since 2002) for the pedagogical universities – 'Media Education' ([1] 03.13.30), and the launch of a new academic journal 'Media Education' (since January 2005), partly sponsored by the ICOS UNESCO 'Information for All'.

Additionally, the Internet sites of Russian Association for Film and Media Education (English and Russian versions) were created. Taking into account the fact that UNESCO defines media education as the priority field of the cultural educational development in the XXI century, media literacy has good prospects in Russia. In North America, the beginnings of a formalised approach to media literacy as a topic of education is often attributed to the 1978 formation of the Ontario Association for Media Literacy (AML). Before that time, instruction in media education was usually the purview of individual teachers and practitioners. Canada is the first country in North America to require media literacy in the school curriculum. Every province has mandated media education in its curriculum. For example, in Quebec the new curriculum mandates media literacy from Grade 1 right up to the final year of secondary school (Secondary V).

The launching of media education in Canada came about for two reasons. One reason was the concern about the pervasiveness of American popular culture and the other was the education system-driven necessity of contexts for new educational paradigms. Media education is less widespread in formal schooling in the United States, in part because of the decentralised nature of the education system in a country with 70 million children now in public or private schools. There is no central authority making nationwide curriculum recommendations, and each of the fifty states has numerous school districts, each of which operates with a great degree of independence from one another. As of 2004, Montana became the first state to develop educational standards around media literacy that students are required to be competent in by grades 4, 8, and 12. Additionally, an increasing number of school districts have begun to develop school-wide programmes, elective courses, and other after-school opportunities for media analysis and production. Nearly all 50 states have language that supports media literacy in state curriculum frameworks.

Leading universities such as Appalachian State University, Columbia University, New York University, the University of Texas-Austin, and Temple University offer courses and summer institutes in media literacy for pre-service teachers and graduate students. Brigham Young University offers a graduate programme in media education specifically for inservice teachers. In South Africa, the increasing demand for Media Education has evolved from the dismantling of apartheid and the 1994 democratic elections.

The first national Media Education conference in South Africa was actually held in 1990 and the new national curriculum has been in the writing stages since 1997. Since this curriculum strives to reflect the values and principles of a democratic society there seems to be an opportunity for critical literacy and Media Education in Languages and Culture courses.

JOURNALISM SCHOOLS

Basically, journalism school is a school or department, usually part of an established university, where journalists are trained. "Journalism is the key to life," said one famous Nebraskan. An increasingly used short form for a journalism department, school or college is 'j-school'. Many of the most famous and respected journalists of the past and present had no formal training in journalism, but learned their craft on the job, often starting out as *copy boys/copy girls*.

Today, in many parts of the world it is usual for journalists to first complete university-level training which incorporates both technical skills such as research skills, interviewing technique and shorthand and academic studies in media theory, cultural studies and ethics. Historically, in the United Kingdom entrants used first to complete a non media-studies related degree course, giving maximum educational breadth, prior to taking a specialist postgraduate pre-entry course. However, this has changed over the last ten years with journalism training and education moving to higher educational institutions. There are now over 60 universities in the UK offering BA honours degrees in journalism. Postgraduate courses are more well-established, some of which are either recognised by the National Union of Journalists (NUJ) or the National Council for the Training of Journalists (NCTJ).

The first programme for journalism education was introduced by former Confederate General, Robert E. Lee, during his presidency at Washington and Lee University, in Lexington, Virginia, in the 1860s. The world's first journalism school was founded by Walter Williams as the Missouri School of Journalism at the University of Missouri in 1908. Since then the journalism school has become standard at most major universities.

Top Journalism Schools

There have been various attempts to rank journalism schools, and the question of which are the "best" or "top" journalism schools is frequently raised on the internet by students. Many institutions claim to be leading schools of journalism, and there is inevitably debate about which are the most appropriate criteria with which to evaluate and judge journalism schools. Awards are obvious indicators of a quality J-school, as are the quality of school graduates.

Australia and New Zealand

In Australia, a ranking of all journalism schools in the country has been assembled based on graduating students' assessments of the quality of their courses: . Top journalism schools in Australia include Jschool and the University of the Sunshine Coast. The New Zealand Training Organisation has published a list of that country's journalism schools recognised by industry.

Europe

The Centre de Formation des Journalistes (CFJ) was founded in 1946 by two Resistance leaders. Located on the rue du Louvre in Paris, many of the leading journalists in France today graduated from this school and come back to help train today's students.

Europe's most long-established postgraduate centre of journalism education is the highly-regarded Department of Journalism at City University, London.

The UK's top-rated course by the National Council for the Training of Journalists is at Nottingham Trent University. Cardiff University, Sheffield, University of Central Lancashire and Kingston University also have well-respected journalism departments. Issues from a European perspective in evaluating journalism schools are discussed by the president of the European Journalism Training Association:

In Russia, the MSU Faculty of Journalism is the leading journalism school. The majority of textbooks on journalism in Russian were written by MSU scientists. In Minsk (Belarus) The Institute of Journalism of BSU is one of the leading scientific and educational centers in the sphere of Mass Media on the territory of the former soviet countries.

It possesses a high scientific and pedagogical potential and it's able to prepare high-qualified professionals of Mass Media ready to work in Belarus and abroad.

Journalism Schools in Colombia

In Colombia, the high court determined in 1998 that

journalism was not a career. This High court said that journalism is a human right, not a profession.

Because of the ruling there are many schools of communications in Colombia where people study to work in mainly enterprises, but not in mass media

There are only two schools of journalism:

> University of Antioquia, a public institution in Medellín, offers Journalsim inside the Communcations faculty. And University of Rosario in Bogotá, a private institution offers Public Opinion Journalism

North America

In the United States the Accrediting Council on Education in Journalism and Mass Communications (ACEJMC) applies nine standards in evaluating university programmes: mission, governance and administration; curriculum and instruction; diversity and inclusiveness; full-time and part-time faculty; scholarship: research, creative and professional activity; student services; resources, facilities and equipment; professional and public service; and assessment of learning outcomes. The ACEJMCC has awarded accreditation to 109 university and college programmes of study in journalism and mass communications, but does not attempt to rank the courses or programmes. It accredits colleges, schools, Departments or "Divisions. The listing of a unit as accredited indicates that the unit has been judged by ACEJMC to meet its standards.

That judgment is rendered after a self-study prepared by the faculty and administration of the unit and an independent evaluation of the unit by educators and practitioners. The listing shows the bachelor's and professional master's degree programmes that were examined during the unit's most recent accreditation review. Some units offer degrees in addition to those listed here. ACEJMC does not accredit programmes leading to the Ph.D., which is considered a research (and not a professional) degree. The Council does not list sequences or specialties.

Editor & Publisher has presented an unranked list of leading journalism schools, while *U.S. News & World Report* produces annual lists of the top schools in advertising, print, and other categories based on responses to questionnaires sent to deans and faculty members. A list based on a variety of resources claims to identify the "ten most popular journalism schools in the United States". One critic has pointed to the anecdotal nature of much j-school ranking in the absence of effective tracking of journalism graduates' career paths. Generally, America's most prominent journalism programmes are considered those at Columbia University, [E.W Scripps School of Journalism | Ohio University]], University of Georgia, Northwestern University, Indiana University:Bloomington and the University of Missouri.

Other well-known programmes include those at Colorado State University, Indiana University, Michigan State University, Syracuse University, Quinnipiac University, University of Florida, University of North Carolina, Chapel Hill, University of Maryland, and University of Illinois at Urbana-Champaign.

On the internet, a range of weblogs have been set up by journalism students to chronicle or to criticize their journalism colleges.

One journalism school in the UK, at the University of Westminster, has established a clearing house where all students are expected to contribute to the development and content of their own education and training using blogs.Various commentaries on journalism education are related to criticisms of contemporary news media standards and values. One example is a paper by Jan Schaffer, executive director of J-Lab: the Institute for Interactive Journalism. A controversial paper to Australia's peak newspaper industry body PANPA (Pacific Area Newspaper Publishers Association) by Professor John Henningham ("Journalism sold short in media courses") blamed industry lack of interest and university cost-cutting for falling standards in journalism education.

Prominent Journalism Schools and Programmes

United States

- Central Michigan University Department of Journalism
- Henry W. Grady College of Journalism and Mass Communication at the University of Georgia
- The Department of Journalism, Roy H. Park School of Communications, Ithaca College
- The College of Communications Department of Journalism at the Pennsylvania State University
- The Department of Journalism at Ball State University
- The College of Communication and Information Sciences at The University of Alabama
- The Department of Journalism at New York University
- Annenberg School for Communication at the University of Southern California, and the University of Pennsylvania
- University of Oregon School of Journalism and Communication

- School of Journalism and Mass Communications at University of South Carolina
- The Edward R. Murrow School of Communication at Washington State University
- Philip Merrill College of Journalism at the University of Maryland
- Columbia University Graduate School of Journalism
- Colorado State University Department of Journalism and Technical Communication
- Gaylord College of Journalism and Mass Communication at the University of Oklahoma
- University of South Carolina (of Journalism and Mass Communication) in Columbia, SC
- S. I. Newhouse School of Public Communications at Syracuse University.
- Ernie Pyle School of Journalism at Indiana University
- E.W. Scripps School of Journalism at Ohio University
- Texas Tech University College of Mass Communications Department of Journalism
- University of Texas School of Journalism
- The Mayborn School of Journalism at University of North Texas
- Michigan State University School of Journalism
- Medill School of Journalism at Northwestern University
- Missouri School of Journalism at University of Missouri
- College of Journalism and Mass Communications at the University of Nebraska–Lincoln

- University of Florida School of Journalism
- UC Berkeley Graduate School of Journalism
- UC Irvine offers an undergraduate degree in Literary Journalism.
- University of Colorado School of Journalism and Mass Communication
- University of Wisconsin-Madison
- University of Iowa Adler School of Journalism
- Walter Cronkite School of Journalism and Mass Communication at Arizona State University
- Boston University College of Communication
- [[School of Journalism and Mass Communication at Kent State University
- School of Journalism and Mass Communication at University of Minnesota
- School of Journalism and Mass Communication at the University of North Carolina at Chapel Hill
- School of Communication at American University
- The Department of Journalism at the University of Arizona
- The Department of Journalism at the University at Albany
- The Department of Journalism and Mass Communications at Washington and Lee University
- College of Communications at University of Illinois Urbana-Champaign
- The Washington Journalism Center in Washington, D.C.

- School of Media and Public Affairs at The George Washington University
- School of Media Arts and Design at James Madison University
- The P. I. Reed School of Journalism at West Virginia University
- School of Journalism Southern Illinois University
- School of Journalism and Broadcasting, Western Kentucky University
- New England School of Communications, Bangor, Maine
- University of Memphis, School of Journalism, Memphis, Tennessee
- School of Journalism University of Montana
- Meadows School of Journalism at Southern Methodist University, Dallas, Texas

Canada

- The Department of Journalism at Concordia University in Montreal, QC.
- University of Western Ontario
- School of Journalism and Communication at Carleton University
- Journalism at Ryerson University
- Journalism at University of Toronto, Scarborough, Joint Programme with Centennial College
- School of Journalism at the University of British Columbia
- Journalism at University of King's College

Latin America

- Colombia: University of Antioquia Journalsim career. Rosario university Public Opinion Journalism
- Chile: Pontificia Universidad Católica de Chile was the first Journalism School outside the US in being acredited by the ACEMJC.

Australia and New Zealand

- Jschool: Journalism Education & Training

University of Technology, Sydney - Journalism Department

Asia

- Indian Institute of Mass Communication (IIMC), New Delhi
- R K Films & Media Academy, New Delhi
- Asian College of Journalism, Chennai
- A J K Mass Communication Research Centre, Jamia, New Delhi
- Department of Journalism, Hong Kong Baptist University
- Institute for Journalism and Society, Hong Kong Baptist University
- Journalism and Media Studies Centre, University of Hong Kong
- Department of Journalism at the College of Mass Communication, University of the Philippines Diliman
- Department of Journalism, College of Communication, Polytechnic University of the Philippines
- Asian Institute of Journalism and Communication

- Department of Journalism, Shih Hsin University, Taiwan
- Department of Journalism, National Chengchi University, Taiwan
- Department of Journalism & Communication Studies, Fu Jen Catholic University, Taiwan
- Division of Journalism & Publishing at Wee Kim Wee School of Communication and Information, Nanyang Technological University, Singapore

Europe

- Nottingham Trent University Centre for Broadcasting and Journalism - Nottingham, England
- CELSA Paris - Sorbonne University, France
- Paris Institute of Political Science - Paris, France
- CFJ Paris-based Journalism School and Training center, Paris, France
- City University Journalism Department - London, England
- JMG, University of Gothenburg - Gothenburg, Sweden
- Leeds University - Institute of Communications Studies - Yorkshire, England
- London College of Communication - University of the Arts, London - London, England
- Moscow State University Faculty of Journalism - Moscow, Russia
- Westminster University Journalism Department - London, England
- Kingston University Journalism Department.

6

News Broadcasting

News broadcasting varionsly, known as newscast or newsbreak the broadcasting of various news events and other information via television or radio. The content is usually either produced locally in a newsroom, or by a broadcast network. It may also include such additional material as sports coverage, weather forecasts, traffic reports, commentary and other material that the broadcaster feels is relevant to their audience.

Categories

1. Television news refers to disseminating current events via the medium of television. "News bulletins" or "newscasts" are programmes lasting from seconds to hours that provide updates on world, national, regional or local news events. Television news is very image-based, showing video of many of the events that are reported. Television channels may provide news bulletins as part of a regularly scheduled news programme. Less often, television shows may be interrupted or replaced by "news flashes" to provide news updates on current events of great importance or sudden events of great importance.

2. Cable news refers to channels which are devoted to current events 24-hours a day. The originator of this format

from which the name derives is CNN (as well as CNN International), which originally stood for cable news network in reference to the then-new phenomenon of cable television. As satellite and other forms have evolved, the term *cable news* has become something of an anachronism but is still in common use; many other channels have since been established, such as BBC World News, BBC News, Sky News, Al Jazeera, France 24, STAR News, Fox News Channel, MSNBC and ABC News Now. Some news channels specialize even further, such as ESPNEWS (sports from ESPN), CNBC, Bloomberg Television and Fox Business Network (financial). A term which has entered common parlance to differentiate cable news from traditional news broadcasts is network news, in reference to the traditional television networks on which such broadcasts air. A classic example is the cable news channel MSNBC, which overlaps with (and, in the case of breaking world-changing events, pre-empts) its network counterpart NBC News.

Television News Channel

Television news channels are television specialty channels which focus on presenting news content. The world's first dedicated 24-hour news channels were CNN and BBC World News.

3. Radio news is the same as television news but is transmitted through the medium of the radio. It is more based on the audio aspect rather than the visual aspect. Sound bites are captured through various reporters and played back through the radio.

News updates occur more often on the radio than on the television - usually about once or twice an hour. At most news/talk radio stations, newscasts run from :00-:06 minutes after the top of each hour. Some stations produce the entire six minutes on their own. Others begin with a network newscast, which covers national and world news, followed by a 2- or 3-minute local newscast. Most of the time, time is taken out of the news "window" for commercials and a weather forecast. In larger cities, traffic reports are also included. Some stations do traffic only during rush hour while others cover traffic around the clock.

Newscasts

Local TV news stations normally broadcast 3-4 times a day: 5:00 & 6:00 in the morning, Noon, 5:00 & 6:00 in the evening, and 10:00 or 11:00 at night. Many stations title their newscasts with catchy names like "Daybreak," "Good Morning (insert city here)," "Live at Five," "Eleven @ 11:00," or "Nightcast." These names are intended to set one station apart from the rest, especially for viewers who are chosen for audience measurement surveys. If the respondent was unable to provide a channel number or call letters, the newscast title is often enough for the appropriate station to receive Nielsen ratings credit.

Radio station newscasts can range from as little as a minute to as much as the station's entire schedule, such as the case of all-news radio.

- More often, AM stations will air a 6 1/2 minute newscast on the top of the hour, which can be either a local report, a national report from a radio network such as CBS Radio or ABC Radio, or a mix of both local and national content, including weather and traffic reports. Some stations also air a two minute report at the bottom of the hour.
- FM stations, unless they feature a talk radio format, usually only air minute-long news capsules featuring a quick review of events and an abbreviated weather

forecast, and usually only in drive time periods or in critical emergencies, since FM stations usually focus more on playing music. Traffic reports also air on FM stations, depending on the market

Remarkably, in some parts of the world there are 'rolling news' TV channels that broadcast news 24 hours a day, such as CNN in the United States or BBC News in the United Kingdom. Many news reports presented on the Internet are updated 24 hours a day. Newscasts consist of several different elements, introduced by a news presenter or presenters. The presenters read 'links' and do interviews. Most news stories come in the form of short 'packages'. These are pre-recorded reports usually lasting from one to five minutes. News reporters gather and edit together interview clips, pictures and their own 'pieces to camera' to tell a story.

They script and record a 'voice-over' to explain the pictures and link the elements together. Some stories are done as live reports. This can be a reporter on the scene of a story either being interviewed by a studio presenter (sometimes known as a 'two-way'), a reporter interviewing one or more other people, or simply live pictures and sound of an event. The sound and pictures are sent back to the TV station via fixed cable links, bounced off a satellite through a satellite truck, or sent through microwave radio transmissions from a vehicle carrying a microwave transmitter.

With the growth of "rolling news" channels the use of live material has increased enormously and TV reporters are now often judged as much on their ability to perform live in front of a camera as on their package-making or writing skills. TV news programmes are put together by producers, who decide what goes in and what gets left out, and how long and in what form each story is presented. They put together 'running orders' - a list of the stories in what they decide is the right order. A separate news editor or assignment editor is often responsible for co-ordinating the gathering of material while a director puts the show together, with help of the technical director, floor director and a crew of people running audio, graphics, teleprompter, and cameras. Most news shows are broadcast live.

The invention of telecommunications and broadcasting has resulted in "the uncoupling of space and time." Spatial distanciation no longer required temporal distanciation. Information can be transmitted over long distances with hardly any delay. Broadcasting, especially news programmes, have changed the way we perceive many people, ideas, jobs, etc. At one time, the leadership and authority of politicians were in awe with everybody. Now that their speeches, actions and decisions are all recorded and broadcast on news programmes, people realised they make mistakes too, and are just like any other person. Not only does TV decrease our awe, it also increases the politician's self-doubt and lowers self-esteem. When giving a speech, we can see the speech-givers nerves and anxiety up close.

Production Management

Theatrical production management is a sub-division of stagecraft. The production management team (consisting of a production manager and any number of assistants) is responsible for realizing the visions of the producer and the director or choreographer within constraints of technical possibility. This involves coordinating the operations of various production sub-disciplines (scenic, wardrobe, lighting, sound, projection, automation, video, pyrotechnics, stage management, etc.) of the presentation. Besides management and financial skills, a production manager must have detailed knowledge of all production disciplines including a thorough understanding of the interaction of these disciplines during the production process.

This may involve dealing with matters ranging from the procurement of staff, materials and services, to freight, customs coordination, telecommunications, labor relations, logistics, information technology, government liaison, venue booking, scheduling, operations management and workplace safety.

REFERENCES

Meyrowitz, Joshua. *Mediating Communication: What Happens?* Ch. 3.

Thompson, John. *The Media and Modernity.* Cambridge, Polity Press, 1995. p 19.

7

Key Media Professionals

> "Precepts or maxims are of great weight, and a few useful ones at hand do more toward a happy life than whole volumes that we know not where to find."
>
> —*Seneca*

In the present chapter we will introduce you some key professionals in Media.

I. MEDIA PROPRIETOR

In fact media proprietor is a person who controls, either through personal ownership or a dominant position in any media enterprise. Those with significant control of a public company in the mass media may also be called "media moguls", "tycoons", "barons", or "bosses".

The figure of the media proprietor first became prominent in the 19th century with the development of mass circulation newspapers.

In the 20th century the definition of proprietorship expanded to include ownership of radio and television networks, as well as film studios, publishing houses and more recently internet and other forms of multimedia companies. The term "press baron" was replaced by "media" baron, reflecting this.

In the *Mogulize Your Business* system, author and creator Damian Skinner defines a Mogul as someone who creates and controls a customer's funnel of experience through three primary points of control: perception, touch points, and exposure.

MEDIA PLANNER

Media Planner is a job title in an advertising agency or media planning and buying agency, responsible for selecting media for advertisement placement on behalf of their clients. The main aim of a Media Planner is to assist their client in achieving business objectives through their advertising budgets by recommending the best possible use of various media platforms available to advertisers. Their roles may include analyzing target audiences, keeping abreast of media developments, reading market trends and understanding motivations of consumers (often including psychology and neuroscience).

Traditionally, the role of the media planner was quite close to that of the *Media Buyer*, the obvious distinction being that the planner would devise a plan for advertising and the buyer would negotiate with the Media proprietor on things such as rates, copy deadlines, placement, merchandising, etc. The role of the modern media planner is more wide reaching however. Today many agencies are actually eschewing the job title of 'media planner' in favour of titles such as communications planner, brand planner or strategist. This reflects the shift away from 'traditional' media planning to a more holistic approach, with the planner now having to consider (as well as standard above-the-line channels such as TV, print, radio and outdoor) PR, below-the-line channels, in-store, digital media, product placement and other emerging communications channels all for the purpose of ensuring the client's advertising budget is well spent as well as adhering to the overall marketing strategy devised by marketing consultants or the client themselves. Their expanded job scope has thus made greater demands of their time, placing them in immensely pressured situations matched by the states faced by their creative (copywriters and art directors) counterparts.

Though many media planners are housed within ad firms, Initiative Worldwide, Carat, ZenithOptimedia, Starcom, Mindshare and OMD are examples of stand-alone global media planning agencies for general consumer brands. As media opportunities grow increasingly fragmented, greater degrees of specificity and specialization have become expected by advertisers. Specialization within individual vertical industries has become the norm. For example, Communications Media Inc. is known for media planning for the pharmaceutical industry, and would therefore be versed in the complex legality of advertising within that industry.

Criterion Global is an international media buyer with expertise in lead-generation media buying, customizing multi-lingual and multi-market media strategy to suit the return on investment objectives of travel, real estate, higher education, and retail brands. Strategic Media, in Washington DC, US specializes in political campaign media buying, which requires special expertise due to legal restrictions on political advertising expenditure and other campaign finance cash-flow regulations. Additionally, specialization within media type has made the media planning landscape more complex.

For example, digital media planners are now heavily recruited by media firms. Future areas of digital specialization with high expected growth rates include: behavioural planning specialists, ad network marketing specialists, social media specialists, and SEO/SEM/PPC experts.

MEDIA CONSULTANT

A media consultant is a term (expression) used to describe a marketing agent or public relations executive, hired by businesses or political candidates to obtain positive press coverage. Media consultants usually draft press releases to highlight positive achievements of a business, organization, or individual. In politics, Media consultants create ads campaigns designed to plant a desired image in the minds of voters.

It is also used to describe a person or company that enables media organisations develop their businesses. An example would be a company that is moving its print business online would need to consult a consultant to aid in this process.

Recently, many consultants have entered the area of social media. Social media consultants' work involves advising clients on developing online media campaigns. These campaigns typically include the use of video, blogs, forums and other features commonly seen on social networking sites.

These consultants also assist companies with managing their online presence on blogs and popular social networking sites such as Facebook, Myspace, Twitter and the like.

Increasingly, the more engaged companies are in social media the more valued their brands are.

NEWS PRODUCER

A news producer is one of the most integral members of any

news-production team. The news producer takes all the elements of a newscast (packages, video, graphics, etc.) and compiles them into a cohesive show.

In the hierarchy of the newsroom, the news producer is under the executive producer, who reports to the news director. The news producer is usually on the same level as the anchor, although this may differ from newsroom to newsroom. The news producer is over the director, studio crew, reporters, field crew, photographers, editors, etc.

Responsibilities

News producers are highly organized and pay extraordinary attention to detail. They thrive in high-stress environments and have good news judgment. They are exceptionally-strong news writers, especially under pressure, and are prepared to write stories with very little notice and in a very short period of time.

The news producer's responsibilities are wide-ranging. In no particular order of importance (because all are equally important), they:

- Write the script for the news anchor(s) to read (though in some Designated Market Areas, the anchor(s) prefer to write this themselves)
- Organize the show, to ensure that there is good "flow"
- Gather leads for possible stories
- Monitor the wire agencies/network feeds for potential stories
- Edit video for voice-overs
- Time the show, so it starts and ends on time, and contains all the commercial breaks necessary

- Communicate with the anchors, director, and studio crew while filming the show
- Keep in touch with reporters and crew in the field in order to monitor how stories are developing
- Write in-show and pre-show teases
- Co-ordinate live shots

PRESS SECRETARY

A press secretary or press officer is a senior advisor who provides advice on how to deal with the news media and, using news management techniques, helps their employer to maintain a positive public image and avoid negative media coverage. They often, but not always, act as the organization's senior spokesperson. Many governments also have press secretaries.

A deputy press secretary is typically a mid-level political staffer who assists the press secretary and communications director with aspects of public outreach. They often write the press releases and media advisories for review by the press secretary and communications director. There are usually assistant press secretaries and press officers that support the press secretary.

PUBLICIST

Basically, publicist is a person whose job is to generate and manage publicity for a public figure, especially a celebrity, a business, or for a work such as a book, film or album. Most top-level publicists work in private practice, handling multiple clients. In the world of celebrities, unlike agents or managers, publicists typically take a monthly fee for serving a client (whereas agents and managers tend to take a percentage of their client's gross income).

Publicists can be at local, regional or national level. They can also have special expertise in areas such as entertainment or literary publicity. One of the publicist's main functions is to generate press coverage on behalf of clients and to serve as the bridge between clients, their public and media outlets. A publicist writes press releases, manages campaigns and performs other public relations functions. It usually takes many years to develop the media contacts, experience and relationships necessary to be an effective publicist.

Some publicists specialize in representing 'ordinary' members of the public to procure the maximum possible fee for stories they wish to sell to newspapers, television stations and magazines.

An older meaning of the term is closer to pamphleteer: someone who circulates ideas by publishing them, perhaps in ephemeral forms.

SENIOR MEDIA CREATIVE

The position senior media creative is found on the advertising agency side as well as on the client side. The senior media creative oversees and develops the creative work of a product launch or product repositioning.

The position senior media creative is comparable to a creative director. Although the senior media creative has to be knowledgeable in more than two or three mass media like television or Internet or print.

The senior media creative is, like a creative director, responsible for the creative lead - building up, leading and motivating the creative team. The senior media creative develops side by side with the client, account director, marketing strategist, planning director, group creative director the vision of the product launch or repositioning. He or she combines all necessary media and professionals to bring this vision to life.

The senior media creative is part of a large professional team, which can include a group creative director, writer, designer, art director, programmer, web developer, account director, marketing director, planner, movie director, composer, producer, animator, traffic coordinator and so forth.

The senior media creative reports to the managing director and group creative director.

Qualifications

Over the years it has shown that a senior media creative need to demonstrate experience in these six areas.

1. Media Knowledge

The senior media creative has to have proven knowledge in the media fields: television, print, online, promotion, marketing, below the line, above the line. Executed television, print, web, promotion work is required.

2. Work Experience on Client Site and Agency Site

The senior media creative must have work experience in a full-time position or as freelancer at the client and agency side - preferably in a global network agency/company.

3. Education: Creative and Business

Due to the fact that the senior media creative is involved in the overall vision of the product launch or repositioning the senior media creative has to have a solid and proven education in the creative and business field. A university degree in communication design or art is required. And additional in-firm training with business schooling is necessary. An international education is common and expected.

4. International Experience

The senior media creative has to have proven international working experience. He or she has to be involved in international campaigns, worked with international clients. Experience within different cultures and work habits is necessary.

5. Work Ethic, Team Player

The senior media creative has to work with all kind of different professionals. It is necessary to be an excellent communicator to creative, IT, business people and so forth. The Media Creative has to be a hands-on team leader.

6. Creative Responsibility

The senior media creative develops side by side with the client, account director, marketing strategist, planning director, creative director the vision of the product launch or repositioning. The senior media creative brings the creative vision down to a simple message. The senior media creative combines all necessary media and professionals to make the product successful.

SHOW RUNNER

Show runner is a term used in the Canadian and United States television industry referring to the person who is responsible for the day-to-day operation of a television series. The term is also occasionally applied to people in the television industries of other countries. Unlike films, where directors are typically in creative control of a production, in episodic television the showrunner usually outranks the director.

Traditionally, the executive producer of a television program was the "chief executive", responsible for the show's production. Over time, the title of executive producer became applied to a wider range of roles, from those responsible for arranging financing to an honorific without actual management duties. The term "show runner" was created to identify the producer who actually held ultimate management and creative authority for the program. The blog (and book) *Crafty Screenwriting* defines *showrunner* as "the person responsible for all creative aspects of the show, and responsible only to the network (and production company, if it's not his production company). The boss. Usually a writer."

Los Angeles Times columnnist Scott Collins describes show runners as:

> Hyphenates," a curious hybrid of starry-eyed artists and tough-as-nails operational managers. They're not just writers; they're not just producers. They hire and fire writers and crew members, develop story lines, write scripts, cast actors, mind budgets and run interference with studio and network bosses. It's one of the most unusual and demanding, right-brain/left-brain job descriptions in the entertainment world....[S]how runners make — and often create — the shows, and now more than ever, shows are the only things that matter. In the "long tail" entertainment economy, viewers don't watch networks. They don't even care about networks. They watch shows. And they don't care how they get them.

Traditionally, the showrunner is the creator or co-creator of the series, but this is not always the case. In long-running shows, often the creator of the show moves on, and day-to-day responsibilities of showrunning falls to other writers or writing teams. *ER*, *The Simpsons*, *The West Wing*, *Star Trek: Deep Space Nine* and *NYPD Blue* are all examples of long-running shows that went through multiple showrunners.

Canada

In the Canadian television industry, many terms generally accrued to writers are currently in dispute. "Showrunner" is one of these terms, with many non-writing producers recently trying to claim the term, as the Canadian TV industry has traditionally been a line-producer driven industry. Many producers, citing the difficulty of getting programs financed and off the ground, look to claim the title for themselves.

In Canada, as writers and producers struggle for primacy, the term showrunner has become a football, with many writers refusing to acknowledge non-writing showrunners, and producers resisting giving "producer" credits to writers. Partly due to this confusion and controversy, in 2007 The Writers Guild of Canada, the union representing screenwriters in Canada, established the Showrunner Award at the annual Canadian Screenwriting Awards, partially to call attention to this fact, and to the role of "writing" as an essential component of the showrunner title. The first "Showrunner Award" was presented to Brad Wright, Executive Producer of *Stargate Atlantis*, and *Stargate SG-1*, in April 2007.

THEATRE PRACTITIONER

Theatre practitioner is a modern term to describe someone who both creates theatrical performances and who produces a theoretical discourse that informs their practical work. A theatre practitioner may be a director, a dramatist, an actor, or—characteristically—often a combination of these traditionally-separate roles.

The term is not ordinarily applied to theatre-makers prior to the rise of modernism in the theatre, instead describing theatre praxis from Stanislavski's development of his 'system', through Meyerhold's biomechanics, Bertolt Brecht's epic and Jerzy Grotowski's poor theatre, down to the present day, with contemporary theatre practitioners including Augusto Boal with his Theatre of the Oppressed, Dario Fo's popular theatre, Eugenio Barba's theatre anthropology and Anne Bogart's viewpoints.

Works Cited

- McCullough, Christopher, ed. 1998. *Theatre Praxis: Teaching Drama Through Practice*. New Directions in Theatre Ser. London: Macmillan. ISBN 0-333-64996-6. New York: St Martin's Press.
- Milling, Jane, and Graham Ley. 2001. *Modern Theories of Performance: From Stanislavski to Boal*. Basingstoke, Hampshire and New York: Palgrave.

EXECUTIVE PRODUCER

An executive producer is a producer who is not involved in any technical aspects of the film making or music process, but who is still responsible for the overall production. Typically an executive producer handles business and legal issues.

Motion Pictures

An executive producer of a motion picture is typically a producer who is sometimes involved with a property that has since been optioned into a film, but has no direct input into the creative process of the film itself, for example, authors of optioned literary works.

In the production of a television show there may be many executive producers listed. Sometimes it may be a situation not unlike the one described above for motion pictures: someone with previous involvement with a particular work, a project's financier, or someone in control of the business aspect of production. Sometimes, this title is conferred upon a celebrity or notable creator who has lent their name to a project to boost its prestige or credibility, as a recognition of newly-acquired industry status, or as a perk to the show's main star or creative force.

However, under the unusual rules for establishing writing credits on television series (where writers are often credited as "producers"), the principal writer is almost always credited as an executive producer rather than the more descriptive title of "head writer."

In television an executive producer might have more power than any other credited crew member — this is the case with the show runner. Generally a show runner (still credited as an executive producer) is the creator of a series and/or an influential staff writer on the show.

Their role is to guide the overall creative progress of the show's story over the course of a season — basically, the de facto creative director of the show — and all creative decisions (from casting to script approval) go through them. Usually, while there may be many credited "producers" and "executive producers" (with varying responsibilities) on a television series, there are just one or two in the position of show runner.

For these reasons, it is not unusual for TV shows to have three sets of "Executive Producers:" Traditional EPs (Production Executives, Financiers, etc.), Head Writer(s), and Show runner(s).

Music

In the music industry, the executive producer of an album is often in control of the business side of production, distribution, and promotion. This role can entail obtaining financing, allocating the budget, etc. At times, the executive producer may also provide artistic input such as which songs are placed in the final cut and the order in which the songs are placed. In this instance, the executive producer is usually someone who has had input in producing some of the tracks on the album. A particular executive producer's name attached to an album is sometimes used as a selling point to distributors.

In some instances, an executive producer can be a person who "discovered" a particular act, or someone who represents an act, either as an agent or a lawyer.

Video Games

The title "executive producer" is not well-defined in the video game industry. It may refer to an external producer, from the publisher, who works with the developer. Sometimes the title is used by the studio head of the developer who created the game.

REFERENCES

Complications Ensue: The Crafty TV and Screenwriting Blog

Denis Higgins. *The Art of Writing Advertising : Conversations with Masters of the Craft:* David Ogilvy, William Bernbach, Leo Burnett, Rosser Reeves (January 2003)

Jack W. Plunkett. Plunkett's Retail Industry Almanac 2008: Retail Industry Market Research, Statistics, Trends & Leading Companies (December 2007), pp"416

Janice Rhoshalle Littlejohn (August 15, 2008). "TV's showrunners outrank directors".

The "Channel Island" column from which the quote was taken was published in November 2007, in the early days of the 2007 Writers Guild of America strike.

Writers Guild of America, TV Writers Booklet #1-final, Chapter Four Executive Producers

8

Creative Media Professionals

"Instead of saying that man is the creative of circumstance, it would be nearer the mark to say that man is the architect of circumstance. It is character which builds an existence out of circumstance. From same material one man builds places, another hovels, one warehouses, another villas; bricks and mortar are mortar and brick until the architect can make them something else.

—*Thomas Carlyle*

Media is an emphatic tool of mass communication. The success of media presentation depends on creativity of many persons.

Here in this chapter we will introduce you to some such creative media professionals who play important role in media.

CREATIVE PROFESSIONAL

A creative professional is a person who is employed for the extraction of skills in creative endeavors. Creative professions include writing, art, design, theater, television, radio, motion pictures, related crafts, as well as marketing, strategy, some aspects of scientific research and development, product development, some types of teaching and curriculum design, and more. Since many creative professionals (actors and writers, for example) are also employed in secondary professions, estimates of creative professionals are often inaccurate. By some estimates, approximately 10 million US workers are creative professionals; depending upon the depth and breadth of the definition, this estimate may be doubled.

Although creative professionals have been a part of the workforce for more than 500 years, several events during the past decade have altered industry and public perception of these workers.

The change in status began in the late 1990s when demand for creative workers was high due to the internet boom. Creative workers found that their talents in graphic and interactive design were valuable, and so, the workers began to develop independent cultures in select cities throughout the world, notably San Francisco, CA; New York City, NY, and Boston, MA. Some smaller cities, such as Austin, TX, and Portland, OR also became centers where creative people found abundant opportunity. This trend has been documented in author Richard Florida's book, The Creative Class.

As the creative workforce has evolved in the post-dot.com era, creative workers have continued to flourish. Daniel Pink's book, A Whole New Mind, describes the transition in American business from information age to conceptual age. Pink describes information-era jobs as expendable and exportable, and offers that the MFA may yield more value for newer American workers than the MBA might generate in today's economy.

The Creative Professional, by Howard Blumenthal, describes the phenomenon from yet another perspective: that of the individual worker now emerging as a serious business professional with specific skills on par with lawyers, accountants, doctors, and other workers who are perceived to be within a special class. The book describes the unique business and career issues for the individual creative worker.

To date, most of the information about this growing phenomenon exists in book form. Many of the ideas and mechanisms are related to changes in copyright law, as described by Lawrence Lessig and Creative Commons.

University education for creative professionals is often presented under older definitions of music, art, and related disciplines, but the processes related to creative thought, particularly as they apply to work, are found in books about cognitive psychology. Author and cognitive thinking researcher Howard Gardner has defined a variety of intelligences related to creative workers. Psychologist Mihaly Csikszentmihalyi has described the process of creative work effectively in several books, including Flow: The Psychology of Optimal Experience. Professors in Business have also started to explore the success factors for creative professionals including Harvard Business School Professor Teresa Amabile who has studied and published research on creative professionals like author John Irving among others.

Corporate research and the development of products and services specifically for creative professionals has started to crop up as companies hire increasing numbers of creative professionals to compete on innovation. Recent changes to corporate slogans are indicative of the trend. In 2003, GE's slogan changed from "We Bring Good Things To Life" to "Imagination at Work" and Hewlett Packard adopted the slogan "Invent." Companies such as Apple, Adobe, Behance, and 37 Signals have started developing and marketing products especially for the creative professional community.

CONTRIBUTING EDITOR

A contributing editor is a magazine job title that varies in responsibilities. Most often, a contributing editor is a freelancer who has proven ability and readership draw. The contributing editor regularly "contributes" articles to the publication, but does not actually edit articles, and the title is largely honorary. At smaller magazines the title may imply a staff member with regular writing responsibility and some editorial duties.

When a "contributing editor" is listed on the title page of a book, the term generally designates a person who has served as some kind of consultant in the book's preparation but who is not responsible for the book's final content. As with magazines, the title may be largely honorary.

MUSIC EDITOR

The music editor is a person in film or other multimedia productions (e.g. video or games) responsible for compiling, editing, and syncing music during the production of a soundtrack.

Among the music editor's roles is creating a "temp track", which is a "mock-up" of the film's soundtrack using pre-existing elements to use for editing, audience previews, and other purposes while the film's commissioned score is being composed.

PANEL OPERATORS

The term panel operator generally relates to any person who is employed to operate a broadcast console. This term is more often used in the radio industry.

Panel operators usually do not have on-air speaking roles, and focus only on presenting the program to air technically. People who operate the panel as well as having a speaking role on a show are often known as anchors. Most music announcers these days operate the panel as well as presenting their shift to air.

Panel operators are usually responsible for (but not limited to) the following duties:

- Keeping talent informed of the show's progress
- Keeping the show on time, and timing out to news and other programming elements
- Playing music, commercials and programming elements at appropriate times
- Operating the on-air telephone system
- Co-ordinating and inserting elements such as traffic reports
- Ensuring that talent microphone levels are acceptable, and switching microphones on and off

Panel operators need to be technically able, good at working under pressure and dealing with talent egos, conscious of time constraints and able to think quickly when something goes wrong. The entire on-air presentation of the show is reliant upon their ability.

PHOTOGRAPHER

Basically, a photographer is a person who takes photographs using a camera. A *professional photographer* uses photography to earn money whilst amateur photographers take photographs for pleasure and to record an event, emotion, place or person. A professional photographer may be an employee, for example of a newspaper, or may contract to cover a particular event such as a wedding or graduation, or to illustrate an advertisement.

Others, including paparazzi and fine art photographers, are freelancers, first making a picture and then offering it for sale or display. Some workers, such as policemen, estate agents, journalists and scientists, make photographs as part of other work. Photographers who produce moving rather than still pictures are often called cinematographers, videographers or camera operators, depending on the commercial context. Photographers are also categorized based on the subjects they photograph. Some photographers explore subjects typical of paintings such as landscape, still life, and portraiture. Other photographers specialize in subjects unique to photography, including street photography, documentary photography, fashion photography, wedding photography, war photography, photojournalism and commercial photography.

The exclusive right of photographers to copy and use their products is protected by copyright. Countless industries purchase photographs for use in publications and on products. The photographs seen on magazine covers, in television advertising, on greeting cards or calendars, on websites, or on products and packages, have generally been purchased for this use, either directly from the photographer or through an agency that represents the photographer. A photographer uses a contract to sell the "license" or use of his or her photograph with exact controls regarding how often the photograph will be used, in what territory it will be used (for example U.S. or U.K. or other), and exactly for which products. An additional contract and royalty would apply for each additional use of the photograph. For example, the photographer may sell the use of one photograph to different companies for use on calendars, cereal boxes, magazines, greeting cards, or many other products, in many countries.

The time duration of the contract may be for one year or other duration. The photographer usually charges a royalty as well as a one-time fee, which may or may not then be deducted from the royalties, depending on the terms of the contract. The contract may be for non-exclusive use of the photograph (meaning the photographer can sell the same photograph for more than one use during the same year) or for exclusive use of the photograph (i.e. only that company may use the photograph during the term). For example, a contract may stipulate non-exclusive use of the photograph on print greeting cards for one year within the United States with a certain up front fee and royalty per unit printed. The contract can also stipulate that the photographer is entitled to audit the company for determination of royalty payments. Royalties vary depending on the industry buying the photograph and the use, for example, royalties for a photograph used on a poster or in television advertising may be higher than the royalty for use on a limited run of brochures. A royalty is also often based on the size the photo will be used in a magazine or book, for example, if it is used as a quarter or half-page photo or full page. Cover photos usually command higher fees than photos used elsewhere in a book or magazine.

Photos taken by a photographer while working on assignment for a magazine or other publication or company often belong to the company or publication, rather than to the photographer, unless stipulated otherwise by contract. Professional portrait and wedding photographers often stipulate by contract that they retain the copyright on wedding photos or portrait photos, so that only they can sell further prints of the photographs to the consumer, rather than the customer reproducing the photos by other means. If the customer wishes to be able to reproduce the photos themselves, they may discuss an alternative contract with the photographer in advance before the pictures are taken, in which a larger up front fee may be paid in exchange for reprint rights passing to the customer.

Even amateur photographers need not give their photos away for free if they are of marketable value. Information about licensing and marketing your photographs, and photo licensing contracts, is available online and in libraries. One can gain an understanding of the business of licensing and protecting photographs by consulting a variety of books and online resources on photograph licensing, and/or by contacting a lawyer who specialises in licensing/royalties, particularly of artwork and photography.

There are major companies who have maintained catalogues of stock photography and images for decades, such as Getty Images and others. Since the turn of the 21st century many online stock photography catalogues have appeared which invite photographers to sell their photos online easily and quickly, but often for very little money, without a royalty, and without control over the use of the photo, the market it will be used in, the products it will be used on, time duration, etc. These online catalogues or the industries using the photograph may then profit from the photo with the photographer making little to no money for his photograph. Because of the difficulty in controlling the use of the photograph after it is passed on the internet, the photographer may never be able to license the photograph again for future use or regain ownership of his photograph.

Photo Sharing

Many people upload their photographs to social networking websites and other websites, in order to share them with a particular group or with the general public. Those interested in legal precision may explicitly release them to the public domain or under a free content license. Some sites, including Wikimedia Commons, are punctilious about licenses and only accept pictures with clear information about permitted use. Some photographers may be concerned that a website can share, distribute, or sell these photographs, and/or that other users may download them for further publication or use. Thus, personal photographs on a social website page may wind up in stockpiles or catalogues containing thousands of images where they are purchased and used without your knowledge.

The profit from the photographs then goes to someone else, and no credit to the photographer. This may be especially disturbing in the case of photos that have family and sentimental value, or other photos which the photographer intended to share but not to give away or sell.

Likewise with photos sent in to contests in magazines or websites. Amateur photographers may submit them, giving their name and story about the pictures and be happy for the photo to be printed free of charge in a particular magazine. But the hundreds or thousands of photos that come into the company's ownership in this way will eventually usually be passed on for other uses either in print or on the internet, with the photographer receiving no payment, notice or credit. Only a contract can protect the photographer's rights. Photographers with such concerns must also research individual companies and publishers before selling their photographs, even with a contract, to ensure that the company has a good record and is in good business standing.

CINEMATOGRAPHER

A cinematographer is one photographing with a motion picture camera (the art and science of which is known as cinematography). The title is generally equivalent to director of photography (DP), used to designate a chief over the camera and lighting crews working on a film, responsible for achieving artistic and technical decisions related to the image. The term cinematographer has been a point of contention for some time now; some professionals insist that it only applies when the director of photography and camera operator are the same person, although this is far from being uniformly the case. To most, cinematographer and director of photography are interchangeable terms. Sometimes, however, the term director of photography can refer to the person who supervises the photography in a videotaped television production. For example, Larry Boelens's credit on the Mikhail Baryshnikov *Nutcracker* was "director of photography", although the production was shot on video.

Responsibilities

The English system of camera department hierarchy sometimes firmly separates the duties of the director of photography from that of the camera operator to the point that the DP often has no say whatsoever over more purely operating-based visual elements such as framing. In this case, the DP is often credited as a lighting cameraperson. This system means that the director consults the lighting cameraman for lighting and filtration and the operator for framing and lens choices.

In the American system, which is more widely adopted, the rest of the camera department is subordinate to the DP, who, along with the director, has the final word on all decisions related to both lighting and framing.

The cinematographer typically selects the film stock, lens, filters, etc., to realize the scene in accordance with the intentions of the director. Relations between the cinematographer and director vary; in some instances the director will allow the cinematographer complete independence; in others, the director allows little to none, even going so far as to specify aperture and shutter angle. Such a level of involvement is not common once the director and cinematographer have become comfortable with each other. The director will typically convey to the cinematographer what they want from a scene visually, and allow the cinematographer latitude in achieving that effect.

Societies and Trade Organizations

An elite group of American cinematographers are members of the American Society of Cinematographers (A.S.C.); this organization represents the upper echelon of talent and is dedicated to the advancement of cinematography. Membership is by invitation only. Equivalents in other countries include the Canadian Society of Cinematographers (C.S.C.), the British Society of Cinematographers (B.S.C.) and the Australian Cinematographers Society (A.C.S.) Members of these organizations are entitled to put designatory letters after their names (eg., M. David Mullen, ASC). There is also a society of Cinematographers in India which includes a wide number of talented Cinematographers. This society is called the Indian Society of Cinematographers (I.S.C.). Members of the I.S.C. include Santhosh Sivan,I.S.C., Ravi K. Chandran, I.S.C., Ramachandra Babu, I.S.C. There are other similar organizations in many countries, including Argentina, France, Germany, Italy, Spain, Iran and India.

In some countries, cinematography is a unionized field. In America, cinematographers (directors of photography, camera operators, camera assistants and still photographers) are represented by the International Cinematographers Guild, Local 600, a division of the labor union International Alliance of Theatrical Stage Employees (IATSE). In Canada, they are represented by IATSE Locals 667 (Eastern Canada) and 669 (Western Canada).

HOME SHOPPING HOST

A home shopping host is the on-air host that partners with guests on television shopping channels, such as HSN, QVC, and ShopNBC. The job of a home shopping host is to introduce new presenters and guests to the television audience, and help these guests explain the values and features of the product being showcased.

Back in 1977, Clearwater, Florida radio station owner Lowell 'Bud' Paxson was collecting money from local companies that advertised on his station. One local company, a hardware store owner, refused payment, insisting that not one single customer had heard the broadcast of his radio advertisements. Paxson and the store owner argued back and forth, eventually coming to a compromise: Instead of a financial payment, the store owner gave Paxson a box filled with electric can openers. Paxson took the box, and returned to the radio station.

When the station's talk radio host, Bob Circosta, was on a newsbreak, Paxson asked Circosta to sell these can openers to his audience. Circosta initially objected, but soon complied with his Paxson's wishes. "I looked at him like he had three heads," Circosta said, recalling the moment. "I thought it would be unethical because I was trying to be a serious host." When Circosta returned to the airwaves, he began describing the can openers and asking listeners to buy them. All 112 can openers were purchased in under an hour.

Sensing the vast profit potential of this concept, Paxson launched a shopping channel on local Tampa cable television, later launching nationwide with the Home Shopping Network. Bob Circosta was the first ever home shopping host to appear on either radio, local television, and national television, eventually selling over 75,000 different products and inventions, netting over 20,000 hours of live airtime, and selling over one billion dollars worth of merchandise in the decades that followed. In addition to Bob Circosta, other early home shopping hosts were Alice Cleveland, Bobbi Ray Carter, Tina Berry, Dan Dennis, John Cremeans, and Lisa Robertson.

COSTUME DESIGNER

A costume designer is a person whose responsibility is to design costumes for a film or stage production. He or she is considered part of the "production team", alongside the director, scenic and lighting designers as well as the sound designer. The costume designer might also collaborate with a hair/wig master or a makeup designer. In European theatre the role is somewhat different as the theatre designer will design both costume and scenic elements.

Costume designers will typically seek to enhance a character's persona, and/or to create an evolving plot of colour, changing social status or period through the visual design of garments and other means of dressing, distorting and enhancing the body - within the framework of the director's vision. At the same time, the designer must ensure that the designs allow the actor to move in a manner consistent with the historical period and enables the actor to execute the director's blocking of the production without damage to the garments. Additional considerations include the durability and washability of garments, particularly in extended runs. The designer must work in consultation with not only the director, but the set and lighting designers to ensure that the overall design of the production works together. The designer needs to possess strong artistic capabilities as well as a thorough knowledge of pattern development, draping, drafting, textiles and costume/fashion history as well as awareness of poise when in period dress, and be sensitive to the creative direction that the performer wants to take his/her character.

Duties

A costume designer creates the look of a character in film , television or in a stage production and in plays.

Costume design is a unionized field. In America, costume designers (and designers and scenic artists) are represented by International Alliance of Theatrical Stage Employes, United Scenic Artists Local 829.

Main Types

Professional costume designers generally fall into three types: freelance, residential, and academic.

- A freelance designer is hired for a specific production by a theatre, dance or opera company, and may or may not actually be local to the theater that he or she is designing for. A freelancer is traditionally paid in three installments: Upon hire, on the delivery of final renderings, and opening night of the production. Freelancers are not obligated to any exclusivity in what projects they are working on, and may be designing for several theatres concurrently.
- A residential designer is hired by a specific theatre, dance or opera company for an extended series of

productions. This can be as short as a summer stock contract, or may be for many years. A residential designer's contract may limit the amounts of freelance work they are allowed to accept. Unlike the freelancer, a residential designer is consistently "on location" at the theater, and is readily at hand to work with the costume studio and his or her other collaborators. Residential designers tend to be more established than strict freelancers, but this is not always the case.

- An academic designer is one who holds professorship at a school. The designer is primarily an instructor, but may also act as a residential designer to varying degrees. They are often free to freelance, as their schedule allows. In the past, professors of costume design were mostly experienced professionals that may or may not have had formal post-graduate education, but it has now become increasingly common to require a professor to have at least a Master of Fine Arts in order to teach.

Both residential and academic designers are generally also required to act as Shop Master or Mistress of an onsite costume shop, in addition to designing productions. In a resident theatre, there is almost always a shop staff of stitchers, drapers, cutters and craft artisans. In an academic environment the shop "staff" is generally students, who are learning about costume design and construction. Most universities require costume design students to work a specified number of hours in the shop as part of their course work.

USA is the union that represents costume designers. Although most professional designers are union members, USA has relatively few collective bargaining agreements with theatres when compared with other theatrical unions. However, most major US opera companies do have CBAs with USA. The majority of union contract work for designers is on a project by project basis, not as a part of Collective Bargaining Agreements with theatrical establishments.

Notable Costume Designers

- Theoni V. Aldredge: *Annie, Barnum, A Chorus Line*
- Bob Mackie: *On the Town*
- Desmond Heeley: *Brigadoon*
- Julie Taymor: *The Lion King*
- Gregg Barnes: *Dirty Rotten Scoundrels*
- Ann Roth: *Assassins*
- Jane Greenwood: *The Scarlet Pimpernel, Once Upon a Mattress*
- Santo Loquasto: *Fosse, Ragtime*
- Susan Hilferty: *Wicked, Spring Awakening*
- Ann Curtis: *Jekyll & Hyde*
- William Ivey Long: *The Producers, Chicago*
- Ann Hould-Ward: *Beauty and the Beast, Dance of the Vampires*
- Willa Kim: *The Will Rogers Follies*
- Gregory Gale: *Urinetown, The Wedding Singer*
- Valentina: *The Philadelphia Story*
- Oleg Cassini: *The Razor's Edge, The Ghost and Mrs. Muir, The Mating Season.*
- Colleen Atwood: *Little Women (1994)*
- Cecil Beaton: *My Fair Lady, Gigi*
- Jenny Beavan: *Howards End, Sense and Sensibility*

- William Travilla: *How to Marry a Millionaire*
- John Bright: *Howards End, Sense and Sensibility*
- Milena Canonero: *A Clockwork Orange*, The Godfather, Part III, *Marie Antoinette*
- Ngila Dickson: *The Lord of the Rings: The Return of the King, The Last Samurai*
- Danilo Donati: *Romeo and Juliet*
- Adrian Greenburg: *The Wizard of Oz*
- Valerie Halverson: *Stargate: Atlantis*
- Julia: *Darling, A Hard Day's Night, Goodbye, Mr. Chips, The Slipper and the Rose*
- Edith Head: *Sabrina (1954), The Sting*
- Dorothy Jeakins: *The Sound of Music*
- Deborah Nadoolman: *Raiders of the Lost Ark, The Three Amigos, Thriller*
- Jean Louis: *From Here to Eternity*
- Orry-Kelly: *An American in Paris, Some Like It Hot, Gypsy*
- Walter Plunkett: *Gone with the Wind, Singin' in the Rain*
- Sandy Powell: *The Wings of the Dove, Shakespeare in Love*
- Ann Roth: *The English Patient*
- Irene Sharaff: *Call Me Madam, Guys and Dolls*
- Theadora van Runkle: *Bonnie and Clyde*
- Hazel Webb-Crozier: *Mickybo and Me, Closing the Ring, Your Highness*

GRAPHIC DESIGNER

In fact, a graphic designer is a professional within the graphic design and graphic arts industry who assembles together images, typography or motion graphics to create a piece of design. A graphic designer creates the graphics primarily for published, printed or electronic media, such as brochures and advertising. They are also sometimes responsible for typesetting, illustration, user interfaces, and web design, or take a teaching position, although these specialties may be assigned to specialists in various graphic design occupations. A core responsibility of the designer's job is to present information in a way that is both accessible and memorable.

A degree or certificate from an accredited trade school is usually, considered essential for a graphic design position. After a career history has been established, though, the graphic designer's experience and number of years in the business are considered the primary qualifications. A portfolio, which is the primary method for demonstrating these qualifications, is usually required to be shown at job interviews, and is constantly developed throughout a designer's career.

One can obtain an AAS, BA, BFA, MFA or an MPhil / PhD in graphic design. Degree programs available vary depending upon the institution, although typical U.S. graphic design jobs require at least some form of degree.

Current graphic designer jobs demand proficiency in one or more graphic design software programs, relevant to the job function, such as proficiency with Adobe Creative Suite. If a web designer, he or she should understand how to work with XML, HTML, and basic web programming scripts. If a print designer, he or she should understand the processes involved in printing to be able to produce press-ready artwork.

Designers should be able to solve visual communication problems or challenges. In doing so, the designer must identify the communications issue, gather and analyze information related to the issue, and generate potential approaches aimed at solving the problem. Iterative prototyping and user testing can be used to determine the success or failure of a visual solution. Approaches to a communications problem are developed in the context of an audience and a media channel. Graphic designers must understand the social and cultural norms of that audience in order to develop visual solutions that are perceived as relevant, understandable and effective.

Graphic designers should also have a thorough understanding of production and rendering methods. Some of the technologies and methods of production are drawing, offset printing, photography, and time-based and interactive media (film, video, computer multimedia). Frequently, designers are also called upon to manage color in different media.

Career

The graphic designer's portfolio in the past fifty years was usually a black book or large binder in which samples of the artist's best printed pieces were carried to show prospective clients or employers. Printed pieces are often protected inside by being mounted on boards or slipped into Acetate sleeves.

Since the 1990's, portfolios have become increasingly computer digitized, and now may be entirely digitized and available on the Internet, or on CD, DVD, or via email.

Graphic design relates heavily to corporate identity, the branding and "persona" of a corporation.

LYRICIST

A lyricist is a writer who specializes in song lyrics. A singer who writes the lyrics to songs is a singer-lyricist. This differentiates from a singer-songwriter, who also composes the song's melody in addition to the lyrics.

Collaboration takes different forms. Some composers and lyricists work closely together on the song, with each having an input into both words and tune. Often a lyricist will fill in the words to a tune already fully written out. Dorothy Fields worked in this way. Lyricists have often added words to an established tune, as Johnny Burke did with the Erroll Garner tune *Misty*. Some partnerships work almost totally independently, for example, Bernie Taupin famously writes lyrics and hands them over to Elton John, who then sets them to music, with minimum interaction between the two men.

Religious Songwriting

In the Christian hymn-singing tradition, many of the best-loved pieces have words written to fit existing melodies. The Christmas carol, *What Child Is This*, had its words set to an old English folk tune that formerly was a lover's lament, Greensleeves. The English composer Ralph Vaughan Williams famously set existing poems, by men like William Cowper and Charles Wesley, to traditional folk tunes to create hymns, many of which he published in the English Hymnal. A different way in which this happened was the marriage of non-related words and tune, a well known example being *The Star-Spangled Banner*, the national anthem of the United States, with words written by Francis

Scott Key strictly as a poem, which was later set to the tune of an old drinking song.

Classical Music

In opera, the librettist is responsible for all text, whether spoken or sung in recitative or aria.

PLAYWRIGHT

In fact, a playwright, also known as a dramatist or dramaturg, is a person who writes dramatic literature or drama. These works are usually written to be performed in front of a live audience by actors. They may also be closet dramas or literary works written using dramatic forms but not meant for performance. The term is not a variant spelling of *"playwrite"*, but something quite distinct: the word *wright* is an archaic English term for a craftsman or builder (as in a *wheelwright* or *cartwright*). Hence the prefix and the suffix combine to indicate someone who has *wrought* words, themes, and other elements into a dramatic form, someone who crafts plays. The homophone with *write* is in this case entirely coincidental.

The earliest playwrights in Western literature with surviving works are the Ancient Greeks. These early plays were written for annual Athenian competitions between playwrights held around the 5th century BC. Such notables as Aeschylus, Sophocles, Euripides, and Aristophanes established forms that are still relied on by their modern counterparts.

The term *playwright* appears to have been coined by Ben Jonson in his Epigram 49, *To Playwright*, as an insult, to suggest a mere tradesman fashioning works for the theatre. He always described himself as a poet, since plays during that time were always written in meter and so regarded as the provenance of poets. This view was held even as late as the early 19th century. The term later lost this negative connotation.

Contemporary playwrights often do not reach the same level of fame or cultural importance that they have in the past, since the theatre is no longer the only outlet for serious drama or entertaining comedies, and must compete with films and television for an audience. In addition, the perilous state of funding for the arts in the U.S. and a growing reliance on ticket sales as a source of income for non-profit theatres has caused many of them to reduce the number of new works they produce. For example, Playwrights Horizons produced only six plays in the 2002-03 seasons, compared with thirty-one in 1973-74. As revivals and large-scale production musicals become the *de rigueur* Broadway (and even Off-Broadway) production, it has become much more difficult for playwrights to make a living in the business, let alone become major successes.

However, the most successful playwrights are often high-status figures in their industry, in stark contrast to the status of the screenwriter in Hollywood. While this may be considered to be a result of the more literary approach that has characterised the theatre since its roots in poetry, it is also because of the hard fact that according to Dramatists Guild, the playwright has the final say on a production — a situation which leaves less room for the director to be as much of an *auteur* as the film director, since the playwright's vision takes precedence.

SCREENWRITER

Screenwriters or scenarists or scriptwriters are people in a film crew who write/create the screenplays from which films and television programs are made. Most screenwriters, such as famous writer Martin Brossollet, start their careers writing on speculation. That means they write without being hired or paid for it. When such a script is sold, it is called a Spec script. Brossollet started writing scripts to movies and tv series when he was 12 years old and attempted to sell them as spec scripts. He now dominates European Television as a full time paid writer for many networks.

Many of them also work as "script doctors", attempting to change scripts to suit directors or studios; for instance, studio management may have a complaint that the motivations of the characters are unclear or that the dialogue is weak.

Script-doctoring can be quite lucrative, especially for the better known writers. David Mamet and John Sayles, for instance, fund the movies they direct themselves, usually from their own screenplays, by writing and doctoring scripts for others. In fact, some writers make very profitable careers out of the script doctoring food chain, being the ninth or tenth writer to work on a piece; in many cases, working on projects that never see exposure to an audience of any size. A few screenwriters have also found work by selling a treatment (approximately 10-30 pages) or synopsis (usually 1-2 pages), of their screenplay even if it isn't completed yet. This is, however, extremely rare.

One of the most important elements in bringing an idea to fruition for a studio to produce is attaching the right screenwriter to the project. Often projects are sold to studios who then assign their own preferred screenwriters to complete the script or write the final draft. Most professional screenwriters in the U.S. are unionized and are represented by organizations such as the Writers Guild of America, East. The WGA is final arbiter on awarding writing credit for projects under its join.

SCRIPT COORDINATOR

Script Coordinator is a role in the production of a film or television series. The script coordinator is responsible for producing each draft of the script and annotating it for ease of use for the production team.

On a television series the script coordinator is responsible for liasing between the writing and production departments. The writers deliver the first draft of a script to the script coordinator who prepares it for the production team and handles any clearance issues. Clearance refers to the need to check the script for potential legal problems and ensure that all names are cleared by the legal department.

The script coordinator must check the draft for proper formatting, spelling, punctuation and continuity before releasing the draft. Once a script has been released other members of the production team offer notes to the writers necessitating revisions to the script. The process of how widely each draft is released (e.g. just to the writers, then to the writers and producers and then to the network) varies from show to show. With each round of revisions the script coordinator must ensure that the changes are clearly marked, re-issue the script and again check the script for errors. Many script coordinators are also responsible for foreign language translations and compiling a show bible that tracks plot points and character introductions as a reference tool. Script coordinator is a distinct role from script supervisor. A script supervisor is responsible for on-set annotation of the script for editing purposes rather than pre-production co-ordination of the script to facilitate production. Script coordinator is a junior role in the writing staff and becoming a full-time writer is considered a promotion from script coordinator.

SENIOR MEDIA CREATIVE

The position senior media creative is found on the advertising agency side as well as on the client side. The senior media creative oversees and develops the creative work of a product launch or product repositioning. The position senior media creative is comparable to a creative director. Although the senior media creative has to be knowledgeable in more than two or three mass media like television or Internet or print.

The senior media creative is, like a creative director, responsible for the creative lead - building up, leading and motivating the creative team. The senior media creative develops side by side with the client, account director, marketing strategist, planning director, group creative director the vision of the product launch or repositioning. He or she combines all necessary media and professionals to bring this vision to life.

The senior media creative is part of a large professional team, which can include a group creative director, writer, designer, art director, programmer, web developer, account director, marketing director, planner, movie director, composer, producer, animator, traffic coordinator and so forth. The senior media creative reports to the managing director and group creative director.

Over the years it has shown that a senior media creative need to demonstrate experience in these six areas.

1. Education: Creative and Business

Due to the fact that the senior media creative is involved in the overall vision of the product launch or repositioning the senior media creative has to have a solid and proven education in the creative and business field. A university degree in communication design or art is required. And additional in-firm training with business schooling is necessary. An international education is common and expected.

2. Media Knowledge

The senior media creative has to have proven knowledge in the media fields: television, print, online, promotion, marketing, below the line, above the line. Executed television, print, web, promotion work is required.

3. Work Experience on Client Site and Agency Site

The senior media creative must have work experience in a full-time position or as freelancer at the client and agency side - preferably in a global network agency/company.

4. International Experience

The senior media creative has to have proven international working experience. He or she has to be involved in international campaigns, worked with international clients. Experience within different cultures and work habits is necessary.

5. Creative Responsibility

The senior media creative develops side by side with the client, account director, marketing strategist, planning director, creative director the vision of the product launch or repositioning. The senior media creative brings the creative vision down to a simple message. The senior media creative combines all necessary media and professionals to make the product successful.

6. Work ethic, Team Player

The senior media creative has to work with all kind of different professionals. It is necessary to be an excellent communicator to creative, IT, business people and so forth. The Media Creative has to be a hands-on team leader.

TECHNICAL WRITER

A technical writer (also referred to as a technical communicator) is a professional writer who designs, writes, creates, maintains, and updates technical documentation—including online help, user guides, white papers, design specifications, system manuals, and other documents. Engineers, scientists, and other professionals may also produce technical writing, usually handing their work to a professional technical writer for proofreading, editing, and formatting. A technical writer produces technical documentation for technical, business, and consumer audiences.

In addition to solid research, language, and writing skills, a technical writer may have skills in:

- Information design
- Information architecture
- Training material development
- Illustration
- Typography

Technical writing may be on any subject that requires explanation to a particular audience. A technical writer is not usually a subject matter expert (SME), but possesses and applies expertise to interview SMEs and conduct research necessary to produce accurate, comprehensive documents. Companies, governments, and other institutions typically hire technical writers not for expertise in a particular subject, but for expertise in technical writing, i.e., their ability to gather information, analyze subject and audience, and produce clear documentation.

A good technical writer creates documentation that is accurate, complete, unambiguous, and as concise as possible. Technical writers create documentation in many forms: printed, web-based or other electronic documentation, training materials, and industrial film scripts.

Technical writers work under many job titles, including *Technical Communicator, Information Developer*, *Data Development Engineer*, and *Technical Documentation Specialist*. In the United Kingdom and some other countries, a technical writer is often called a *technical author* or *knowledge author*.

Technical writers normally possess a mixture of technical and language abilities. They may have a degree or certificate in technical communications. Many technical writers switch from another technical field such as engineering or science, often after learning the required skills through technical communications classes.

A good technical writer has the ability to create, assimilate and convey technical material in a concise and effective manner. A technical writer may specialize in a particular area. For example, API writers mostly work on API documents, while other technical writers specialize in electronic commerce, manufacturing, scientific or medical material. To create a technical document, a technical writer gathers information by studying existing material and interviewing SMEs. The technical writer also studies the audience to learn their needs and technical level.

Well-formed technical documents follow common publishing guidelines. Technical documentation comes in many styles and formats, depending on the medium. Printed documentation has different standards from online documentation. Usually, technical writers follow formatting conventions described in a standard style guide. In the US, most technical writers use the Chicago Manual of Style (CMS). Many companies have their own corporate style guides, typically extensions of the CMS that cover specific corporate issues. The Microsoft Manual of Style for Technical Publications is typical of these. Engineering projects, particularly defense or aerospace related projects, often follow national and international documentation standards—such as ATA100 for civil aircraft, or S1000D for defense platforms.

Technical writers often work as part of a writing or project development team. Typically, the writer finishes a draft and passes it to one or more SMEs who conduct a *technical edit* to review it for accuracy and completeness. In some cases the writer or others test the document on audience members. On a project team, a technical writer develops the overall project documentation, as other members of the team develop other areas of the project. For example, as engineers design and integrate a system, the technical writer generates the manuals that go with the system.

Career

A technical writer has no standard career path, but technical writers may move into project management over other writers. A writer may advance to a senior technical writer position, handling complex projects or a small team of writers and editors. In larger groups, a documentation manager might handle multiple projects and teams.

Technical writers may also gain expertise in a particular technical domain and branch out into related forms, such as software quality analysis or business analysis. A technical writer who becomes a subject matter expert in a field may transition from technical writing to analyst work in that field.

Senior writers in some software documentation departments are increasingly called *Individual Contributor* (IC). In API/software documentation, ICs typically work with a team of developers or testers across many physical locations. In such software development in "software research organizations," an IC plays an important role in the delivery of API/Software documentation.

UNIT STILL PHOTOGRAPHER

Basically, a unit still photographer or simply, stills photographer is a person who creates still photographic images specifically intended for use in the marketing and publicity of feature films in the motion picture industry and network television productions.

Using individual frames from recorded video material is not practical due to the quality. Much higher resolution images are therefore used. Typically the end uses of these still photos would include the films theatrical release poster, DVD box artwork, the official web site photos, billboards, bus stop adverts, point of purchase displays, key-art image sets released to the press and media as well as other printed and online collateral materials.

Unit still photographers are also responsible for creating "photo props" and "set dressing images", the photos and images used on-camera to create various illusions such as forensic photos, crime drama booking photos, character drivers' licenses, passport & I.D. photos, on-screen family photos, surveillance photos, computer screen displays, and any other image a producer may require in the course of a production.

In North America in particular, and some international locations as well, a Unit still photographer must be a member of IATSE Local 600 International Cinematographers Guild, in order to perform services on Union productions and Union studio lots and locations. The most prestigious of these Unit Still photographers are also members of The Society of Motion Picture Still Photographers, an organization which promotes the work of those within the industry.

While often perceived as a "glamor" job for photographers, the reality is often very long hours (70+ hour weeks are the norm) on remote distant locations under difficult and often extreme conditions. The Unit still photographer often coordinates with the Unit publicist, but physically works in very close proximity not only to the film's camera crew, director, producers and actors, but also by extension in close proximity to the film's boom microphone operator. As such, Unit still photographers go to great lengths to reduce, muffle, and otherwise mute the sound of their camera's motor drive & shutter so as not to distract the actors and to remain inaudible on the film's recorded dialogue soundtrack while the action is rolling. Believe it or not photography is and can be a difficult profession.

Typically this is accomplished using a sound blimp, which is a sound absorbing, foam filled metal case in which the still camera body is fitted with a proprietary remote operation cable. This allows the camera to be activated and operated from a two-button (activation, focus & shutter release) exterior control. Limitations exist once the blimp is closed around the camera as you can no longer access the cameras controls (F-number, shutter speed, ASA/ISO settings) or menu displays, directly. The LCD display will also be out of view to review your images, in the closed position. This requires the photographer to make his control selections in advance, and then stick with those settings until the take-in-progress has been "cut", making adjustments between takes or set-ups. Unit still photographers in this field typically produce over 2000+ marketable images per week for their major studio clients. The use of still photography is the use of alignment, positioning, as well as other techniques used to capture the "money shot." Still life photography is the depiction of inanimate subject matter, most typically a small grouping of objects that are either human-made or natural.

SPECIAL EFFECTS SUPERVISOR

It is pertinent to note that a special effects supervisor (also referred to as a special effects coordinator) is an individual who works on a commercial, theater, television or film set creating special effects. The supervisor generally is the department head who defers to the film's director and/or producers, and who is in charge of the entire special effects team. Special effects include anything that is manual or mechanically manipulated (also called "practical effects" or in camera effects). This may include the use of mechanized props, special effects makeup, props, scenery, scale models, pyrotechnics and atmospheric effects: creating physical wind, rain, fog, snow, clouds etc.

Special effects (SFX) or (SPFX) are produced on the set, as opposed to those created in post-production which are generally called "visual effects" (VFX). In recent years real physical special effects have been largely overshadowed by computer-generated imagery (CGI) effects created in post-production."

THEATRE PRACTITIONER

Theatre practitioner is a modern term to describe someone who both creates theatrical performances and who produces a theoretical discourse that informs their practical work. A theatre practitioner may be a director, a dramatist, an actor, or—characteristically—often a combination of these traditionally-separate roles.

The term is not ordinarily applied to theatre-makers prior to the rise of modernism in the theatre, instead describing theatre praxis from Stanislavski's development of his 'system', through Meyerhold's biomechanics, Bertolt Brecht's epic and Jerzy Grotowski's poor theatre, down to the present day, with contemporary theatre practitioners including Augusto Boal with his Theatre of the Oppressed, Dario Fo's popular theatre, Eugenio Barba's theatre anthropology and Anne Bogart's viewpoints.

BROADCAST DESIGNER

Broadcast designer is a person who designs the graphics and media incorporated in television productions. A broadcast designer may have a degree in Digital Media (or a similar degree), or is self-taught in the software needed to create such content. A large portion of broadcast design is known as "branding" for television channels and programs. The job of the designer is to create a look and feel for a specific idea or subject. Often, television stations will wish to re-invent their style — this is where the broadcast designer's skills are called upon.

Notably, another industry which is reliant on a designer's skill is the commercial market. Most often, a client will hire an advertising agency which will then hire a group of designers to produce a commercial for their product. The process usually begins with a concept or an idea which the client has or the agency comes up with. It is then further explored in design boards which go up for approval by the client before the process of making it actually begins.

REFERENCES

Alexis Soloski, "The Plays What They Wrote: The Best Scripts Not Yet Mounted on a New York Stage", *The Village Voice*, May 21 - 27, 2003

Brothers and Sisters script coordinator Oscar Balderrama on his role

Buffy the Vampire Slayer script coordinator Tamara Becher on her role

Burton, S (2007). "From the executive director: Confronting change" (pdf). http://www.stc.org/PDF_Files/myjob/susanBurton02.pdf. Retrieved 2009-09-23.

CSI Miami producer Corey Miller on the script coordinator role

Denis Higgins. The Art of Writing Advertising : Conversations with Masters of the Craft: David Ogilvy, William Bernbach, Leo Burnett, Rosser Reeves (January 2003)

Fraser, Neil. "Theatre History Explained", *The Cowood Press*, 2004, page 11

IMDB Glossary letter "S": Special Effects Supervisor

In Plain Sight & *Three Rivers* script coordinator Gregory Bonsignore on his role

Jack W. Plunkett. Plunkett's Retail Industry Almanac 2008: Retail Industry Market Research, Statistics, Trends & Leading Companies (December 2007), pp"416

Jessica Helfand. "What is graphic design?". *AIGA*. http://www.aiga.org/content.cfm/what-is-design. Retrieved 2009-06-29. "it is the art of visualizing ideas"

Jonson, Ben, *The Works of Ben Jonson*, Boston: Phillips, Sampson, and Co., 1853. page 788

Lost script coordinator Gregg Nations on his role

Mallory Stark and Martha Lagace (2001). "John Irving's Lessons for Business". President and Fellows of Harvard College. http://hbswk.hbs.edu/item/2000.html. Retrieved 2007-05-28.

Michael McCarthy (2003). "'Imagination at Work' for GE". USA TODAY. http://www.usatoday.com/money/advertising/adtrack/2003-05-04-ge_x.htm. Retrieved 2007-05-28.

NASAD Competencies Summary, BFA in Graphic Design, page 2 http://aqresources.arts-accredit.org/site/docs/AQ-AD/BFA-GraphicDesign.pdf last accessed 29 Jun 2009

NASAD Competencies Summary, BFA in Graphic Design, page 2 http://aqresources.arts-accredit.org/site/docs/AQ-AD/BFA-GraphicDesign.pdf last accessed 29 Jun 2009

Ronald H. Sadoff (2006). "The role of the music editor and the 'temp track' as blueprint for the score, source music, and scource music of films".

[*Courtesy:* Wikipedia]

Appendix

JOURNALISM ETHICS POLICY OF THE NEW YORK TIMES COMPANY

Introduction and Purpose

1. The Core Purpose of The New York Times Company is to "enhance society by creating, collecting and distributing high-quality news, information and entertainment." The central place of our news and editorial units in fulfilling that promise is underscored by the No. 1 statement in our Core Values: "Content of the highest quality and integrity: This is the basis for our reputation and the means by which we fulfill the public trust and our customers' expectations."

2. Companywide, our goal is to cover the news impartially and to treat readers, news sources, advertisers and all parts of our society fairly and openly, and to be seen as doing so. The reputation of our company rests upon that perception, and so do the professional reputations of its staff members. Thus the company, its separate business units and members of its newsrooms and editorial pages share an interest in avoiding conflicts of interest or any appearance of conflict.

3. Conflicts of interest, real or apparent, may arise in many areas. They may involve tensions between journalists' professional obligations to our audience and their relationships with news sources, advocacy groups, advertisers, or competitors; with one another; or with the company or

one of its units. And at a time when two-career families are the norm, the civic and professional activities of spouses, household members and other relatives can create conflicts or the appearance of them.

4. In keeping with its solemn responsibilities under the First Amendment, our company strives to maintain the highest standard of journalistic ethics. It is confident that its staff members share that goal. The company and its units also recognize that staff members should be free to do creative, civic and personal work and to earn extra income in ways separate from their work in our organization. Before engaging in such outside activities, though, staff members should exercise mature professional judgment and consider the stake we all have in the irreplaceable good name of our company and its newsrooms.

The Scope of This Policy

5. These guidelines generally apply to all members of our news and editorial departments whose work directly affects our content and its reputation, including those on leaves of absence. They include writers, reporters, columnists, editors, producers, editorial writers, photographers, picture editors, art directors, artists, designers, graphics editors and researchers. This group also includes News Service and syndication personnel and the shared technical staffs of broadcast and online operations to the extent that those staffs plan, create, transmit or oversee news or editorial content. This entire group of professional journalists is what this document means by "staff" or "staff members."

6. These guidelines are intended to shield the integrity not just of our journalists but of our journalism over all. For that reason, the provisions limiting political activity or

partisanship apply also to publishers and to their counterparts in online and broadcast operations — that is, the executives to whom the chief editors of news and editorial staffs directly report. These specific provisions are detailed in Paragraph 88 below.

7. At the discretion of management in each of our news or editorial departments, the professional journalist guidelines may also be applied to news clerks, administrative assistants, secretaries and other support staff members whose work influences our content. Whether or not a newsroom's management applies these guidelines to the support staff, however, support people are always governed by two important provisions:

- First, no newsroom or editorial page employee may exploit for personal gain any nonpublic information acquired at work, or use an association with our news organization to gain favor or advantage.
- And second, no one may do anything that damages our news staffs' reputation for strict neutrality in reporting on politics and government; in particular, no one may wear campaign buttons or display any other form of political partisanship while on the job.

8. Our contracts with freelance contributors require them to avoid conflicts of interest, real or apparent. In keeping with that provision, they must honor these guidelines in their Times Company assignments, as set forth in Section C below. Similarly, the makers of television or online productions intended to bear our name or to be distributed through our outlets must comply with the policies in this document while working on those projects.

9. At each site in our company, newsroom management will obtain legal opinions on any statutes that may constrain

the enforcement of these guidelines. In those units covered by collective bargaining agreements with the Newspaper Guild, management will obtain legal opinions on any limitation arising from those agreements.

The Nature of This Policy

10. Our fundamental purpose is to protect the impartiality and neutrality of the company's newsrooms and the integrity of their news reports. In many instances, merely applying that purpose with common sense will point to the ethical course. Sometimes the answer is self-evident: simply wondering whether a course of action might damage the reputation of our journalism is often enough to gauge whether the action is appropriate.

11. Every staff member is expected to read these rules carefully and to think about how they might apply to his or her duties. A lack of familiarity with their provisions cannot excuse a violation; to the contrary, it aggravates the violation. The provisions presented here can offer only broad principles and some examples. No written document could anticipate every possibility. Thus we expect staff members to consult their local newsroom management if they have doubts about any particular situation or opportunity covered by this set of rules. In most cases an exchange of e mail should suffice.

12. The company and its units believe beyond question that our staff shares the values these guidelines are intended to protect. Ordinarily, past differences of view over applying these values have been resolved amiably through discussion. The company has every reason to believe that such a pattern will continue. Nevertheless, the company views any intentional violation of these rules as a serious offense that may lead to disciplinary action, potentially including

dismissal, subject to the terms of any applicable collective bargaining agreement.

13. This document is not an exhaustive compilation of all situations that may give rise to an actual or perceived conflict of interest. It does not exclude situations or issues giving rise to such conflicts simply because they are not explicitly covered within this document, nor does the document or any of its particular provisions create an implied or express contract of employment with any individual to whom the guidelines apply. The company reserves the right to modify and expand the guidelines from time to time, as it deems appropriate.

14. The authority to interpret and apply these guidelines is vested in the head of each news or editorial department in the company. That duty may be delegated to their ranking assistants, but the senior news executives remain responsible for decisions made in their name.

Other Standards of Behavior

15. This document embodies basic standards of journalistic conduct applicable across our company. Our operating units are free to adopt further or more detailed policies, such as the specialized standards and practices of the networks with which our broadcast stations are affiliated, or the rules of certain newspapers for reporters' use of unidentified sources. In case of conflict, the policy with the higher standard shall apply.

16. As employees of the Times Company and its units, we observe the Rules of the Road, which are the axiomatic standards of behavior governing our dealing with colleagues and going about our work. Copies are available from management offices in all units. Together with a statement of supporting principles, the rules are on the Internet at

http://www.nytco.com/mission.html. We also observe the company's policies against harassment and on the use of computers and digital communications, which appear on the business ethics page of this site: http://www.nytco.com/business-ethics.html.

A. On the Job

A1. Our Duty to Our Audience

17. As journalists we treat our readers, viewers, listeners and online users as fairly and openly as possible. Whatever the medium, we tell our audiences the complete, unvarnished truth as best we can learn it. We correct our errors explicitly as soon as we become aware of them. We do not wait for someone to request a correction. We publish corrections in a prominent and consistent location or broadcast time slot.

18. We treat audience members no less fairly in private than in public. Anyone who deals with our public is expected to honor that principle, knowing that ultimately our readers and viewers are our employers. Civility applies whether an exchange takes place in person, by telephone, by letter or by e-mail.

19. We gather information for the benefit of our audience. Journalists at the Times Company, or on assignment for one of its newsrooms, may not use their position to make inquiries for any other purpose.

20. Staff members or outside contributors who plagiarize betray our fundamental pact with our public. So does anyone who knowingly or recklessly provides false information or doctored images for publication. We will not tolerate such behavior.

A2. How We Gather the News

21. We treat news sources fairly and professionally.

We do not inquire pointlessly into someone's personal life. We do not threaten to damage uncooperative sources, nor do we promise favorable coverage in return for cooperation. We do not pay for interviews or unpublished documents: to do so would create an incentive for sources to falsify material and would cast into doubt the genuineness of much that we publish.

22. Staff members and others on assignment for us should disclose their identity to people they cover, though they need not always announce their occupation when seeking information normally available to the public. Those working for us as journalists may not pose as anyone they are not — for example, police officers or lawyers.

23. Critics and other writers who review performances or goods and services offered to the public may conceal their press identity, but they may not normally assert a false identity or affiliation. As an exception, restaurant critics may make reservations in false names to avoid special treatment. For that same reason, restaurant critics and travel writers should conceal their affiliation.

Keeping Our Detachment

24. Relationships with sources require sound judgment and self-awareness to prevent the fact or appearance of partiality. Cultivating sources is an essential skill, often practiced most effectively in informal settings outside of normal business hours. Yet staff members, especially those assigned to beats, must be aware that personal relationships with news sources can erode into favoritism, in fact or appearance. Editors, who normally have a wide range of relationships, must be especially wary of showing partiality. Where friends and neighbors are also newsmakers, journalists must guard against giving them extra access or a more

sympathetic ear. When practical, the best solution is to have someone else deal with them.

25. Though this topic defies firm rules, it is essential that we preserve professional detachment, free of any hint of bias. Staff members may see sources informally over a meal or drinks, but they must keep in mind the difference between legitimate business and personal friendship. A city editor who enjoys a weekly round of golf with a city council member, for example, risks creating an appearance of coziness. So does a television news producer who spends weekends in the company of people we cover. Scrupulous practice requires that periodically we step back and look at whether we have drifted too close to sources with whom we deal regularly. The test of freedom from favoritism is the ability to maintain good working relationships with all parties to a dispute.

26. Romantic involvement with a news source would create the appearance and probably the reality of partiality. Staff members who develop close relationships with people who are likely to figure in coverage they prepare or oversee must disclose those relationships privately to a responsible newsroom manager. In some cases, no further action may be needed. But in other instances staff members may have to recuse themselves from certain coverage. Sometimes assignments may have to be modified or beats changed.

Obeying the Law

27. Staff members and others on assignment for us must obey the law in the gathering of news. They may not break into buildings, homes, apartments or offices. They may not purloin data, documents or other property, including such electronic property as databases and e-mail or voice-mail messages. They may not tap telephones, invade

computer files or otherwise eavesdrop electronically on news sources. In the case of government orders or court directives to disclose a confidential source, journalists will consult with the newsroom management and the legal department on the application of this paragraph.

28. Journalists who obtain press cards, press license plates, parking permits or other identification from police or other official agencies may use those credentials only to do their jobs. Those whose duties do not require special credentials must return them.

29. Staff members may not record private conversations without the prior consent of all parties to the conversations. In jurisdictions where recordings made secretly are legal, only the top manager of a news department may make an exception to this rule, and only after consultation with our legal department. Except in limited circumstances, we do not use hidden cameras; any exceptions should first be discussed with the top newsroom manager and the legal department.

Paying Our Own Way

30. When we as journalists entertain news sources (including government officials) or travel to cover them, our company pays the expenses. In some business situations and in some cultures, it may be unavoidable to accept a meal or a drink paid for by a news source (for example, at an official's residence or in a company's private dining room). Whenever practical, however, we should avoid those circumstances and suggest dining where we can pay our share (or, better, meeting in a setting that does not include a meal). Routine refreshments at an event like a news conference are acceptable, but a staff member should not attend recurring breakfast or lunch meetings unless our

company pays for the journalist's meals. Whether the setting is an exclusive club or a service lodge's weekly luncheon, we should pay our way.

31. Staff members may not accept free or discounted transportation and lodging except where special circumstances give little or no choice. Such special cases include certain military or scientific expeditions and other trips for which alternative arrangements would be impractical — for example, an interview aboard a corporate jet where there is no benefit other than the interview. Journalists should consult responsible newsroom managers in advance when special circumstances arise.

32. If permitted by the local newsroom policy, staff members may accept press passes or free tickets when explicitly assigned to review artistic performances or cover athletic and similar events (for example, auto shows, agricultural fairs or flower shows). But no staff member except the assigned one — not even an editor in the arts, feature or sports department — may accept free tickets. And even when paying the box office price, a journalist may not use membership on our staff to obtain scarce seats unless the performance has a clear bearing on his or her job.

Dealing With Competitors

33. We compete zealously but deal with competitors openly and honestly. We do not invent obstacles to hamstring their efforts. When we first use facts originally reported by another news organization, we attribute them.

34. With the exception of press pool arrangements imposed by news sources, staff members may not join teams covering news events for other organizations (unless their work is part of a duly authorized joint venture), and

they may not accept payment from competitors for news tips. They may not be listed on the masthead of any publication or Web site outside our company (except for a nonprofessional publication such as a religious congregation's newsletter, an alumni magazine or a club bulletin).

A3. Protecting Our Neutrality

35. Staff members and those on assignment for us may not accept anything that could be construed as a payment for favorable coverage or for avoiding unfavorable coverage. They may not accept gifts, tickets, discounts, reimbursements or other benefits from individuals or organizations covered (or likely to be covered) by their newsroom. Gifts should be returned with a polite explanation; perishable gifts may instead be given to charity, also with a note to the donor. In either case the objective of the note is, in all politeness, to discourage future gifts.

36. Staff members and those on assignment for us may not accept employment or compensation of any sort from individuals or organizations who figure in coverage they are likely to provide, prepare or supervise. The senior executive of each newsroom may authorize reasonable exceptions (for example, to let a teacher work part time as a copy editor).

37. If local policies permit journalists to share in fees for re-use of certain content, a cap must be set on any payment for advertising or promotional re-use, to avoid the appearance of an incentive for favorable coverage. The journalist's share of such fees may not exceed $200 an article.

38. Staff members may normally accept those gifts or discounts available to the general public. Normally they are also free to take advantage of conventional corporate

discounts that our company shares with all employees (for example, corporate car rental rates). Journalists may accept free museum admissions or other benefits that are offered to all employees as a result of the company's charitable activities. Overseas, our staff may accept museum admissions and similar modest benefits customarily extended to journalists nationally or regionally as an occupational class rather than as individuals.

39. Unless the special terms are offered by The New York Times Company or its subsidiaries or affiliates, staff members may not buy stock in initial public offerings through "friends and family" plans where any plausible appearance of conflict of interest exists. Staff members may not accept allocations from brokerage firms.

Steering Clear of Advice Roles

40. It is an inherent conflict for a journalist to perform public relations work, paid or unpaid. Staff members may not counsel individuals or organizations on how to deal successfully with the news media. They may not, for example, advise candidates for public office, write or edit annual reports, or contribute to the programs of sports teams.

41. They may, of course, explain the newsroom's normal workings and steer outsiders to the appropriate editor or reporter. They may offer basic advice to community or neighborhood institutions such as their child's school, a small museum, a local charity or their house of worship.

42. They should not take part in public relations workshops that charge admission or imply privileged access to the press, or participate in surveys asking their opinion of an organization's media relations or public image. But on occasion they may describe our procedures to public

relations groups with the goal of improving the flow of pertinent information.

43. Staff members may not serve as ghostwriters or co-authors for people or groups who figure in coverage they are likely to provide, prepare or supervise. They may not undertake such assignments for organizations that espouse a cause.

44. Staff members may not engage in financial counseling (except through the articles they write). They may not manage money for others, offer investment advice, or help operate an investment company of any sort, with or without pay. They may, however, help family members with ordinary financial planning and serve as executors or administrators of estates of relatives and friends and as court-appointed conservators and guardians.

Entering Competitions and Contests

45. Staff members may not enter local, national or international competitions sponsored by individuals or groups who have a direct interest in the tenor of our coverage. They may not act as judges for these competitions or accept their awards. Common examples are contests sponsored by commercial, political or professional associations to judge coverage of their own affairs. Senior newsroom managers may make exceptions for competitions underwritten by corporate sponsors if those are broad in scope and independently judged by journalists or disinterested public figures.

46. Staff members may compete in competitions sponsored by groups whose members are all journalists or whose members demonstrably have no direct interest in the tenor of coverage of the field being judged. Staff members

may act as judges for such competitions and accept their awards. For example, a staff member may enter a university-sponsored competition for coverage of foreign affairs but not accept an advocacy group's prize for environmental coverage.

47. Each newsroom's management should maintain a current list of competitions it has approved. Staff members who would like to enter others should consult the responsible news executive. A critical factor in approving a competition, whatever the sponsorship, is a record of arm's-length decisions, including a willingness to honor unfavorable reporting. Staff members who win unsought awards from groups that do not meet the criteria established here should decline, politely explaining our policy.

48. Normally staff members are free to accept honorary degrees, medals and other awards from colleges, universities and other educational institutions. Those who cover higher education or supervise that coverage should be sensitive to any appearance of coziness or favoritism. Those in any doubt should consult their newsroom management before accepting such an award.

Barring Collaboration and Testimonials

49. Staff members and others on assignment for us may not collaborate in ventures with individuals or organizations that are likely to figure in their coverage. Among other things, this prohibition applies to writing books, pamphlets, reports, scripts, scores or any other material and to making photographs or creating artwork of any sort.

50. Staff members may not offer endorsements or testimonials for books, films, television programs or any other programs, products or ventures. They may not accept

endorsements or testimonials from anyone who is likely to figure in their coverage. Newsroom management may authorize rare exceptions (for instance, when a staff member has become expert in a field remote from his or her duties).

A4. Cautions on Public Speaking

51. Speaking before community audiences or educational groups can benefit our company by helping the public understand what we do. But before appearing before an outside group, we must be sure we are not likely to create an actual or apparent conflict of interest or undermine public trust in the impartiality of our journalism.

52. Staff members should be sensitive to the appearance of partiality when they address groups that might figure in their coverage, especially if the setting might suggest a close relationship to the sponsoring group. Before accepting such an invitation, a staff member must consult with newsroom management. Generally, for example, an editor who deals with political campaigns might comfortably address a library gathering but not appear before a civic group that endorses issues or candidates. An environmental reporter can appropriately speak to a horticultural society but not to conservation groups known for their efforts to influence public policy.

53. To avoid an appearance of undue closeness, staff members may not accept invitations to speak before a single company (for example, at a corporate executive retreat) or an industry assembly (such as organized baseball's winter meeting) unless newsroom management agrees that the appearance is useful and does not undermine our reputation for impartiality. In such a case, our company should pay any expenses; no speaker's fee should be accepted.

54. Staff members should not accept invitations from

outside our company to speak where their function is to attract customers to an event primarily intended as profit-making.

Restricting Speaker's Fees

55. Where permitted by local policy, staff members who deliver speeches may accept fees, honorariums, expense reimbursement and free transportation, but only from educational or other nonprofit groups for which lobbying and political activity are not a major focus. A staff member must consult with newsroom management before accepting a substantial speaking fee. Threshold amounts will be determined by local management.

56. Any staff member who accepts fees, honorariums or expenses for speaking engagements must file an annual accounting with newsroom management. (In the case of the top newsroom executive, the accounting is filed with the chief executive of the business unit.) Each unit may set a threshold below which annual accounting is not required. Fees earned under our company's auspices need not be included.

57. A staff member who writes a book and wishes to promote it on personal time must make every effort to ensure that public appearances conform to the spirit of these guidelines and do not interfere with normal job responsibilities. If the staff member has doubts about an appearance, he or she must consult with newsroom management. Routine expenses and fees may be accepted for such promotional appearances. Speeches and other outside activities by staff members, paid or unpaid, should not imply that they carry the endorsement of our company or any of its units (unless they do). On each such occasion, the staff member should gracefully remind the audience

that the views expressed are his or her own. Outside commitments should not interfere with the speaker's normal responsibilities. Thus no staff member should set an extensive speaking schedule without approval from newsroom management.

A5. Rules for Specialized Departments

Sports

58. No member of a sports staff in our company may gamble on any sports event, except for occasional recreational wagering in a legal setting.

59. Except for properly issued press passes for event coverage, members of the sports staff may not accept tickets, travel expenses, meals, gifts or any other benefit from teams or promoters. (At their discretion, unit newsroom managements may permit journalists to accept the light refreshments routinely offered in press boxes during games.)

60. Sports reporters assigned to cover games may not serve as scorers.

Entertainment and the Arts

61. Staff members covering entertainment and the arts have a special duty to guard against conflicts of interest, real or apparent. Arts coverage, whether national or local, can often make or break reputations and commercial success. In theater, movies, music, art, dance, publishing, fashion and restaurants, critics and reviewers have an obligation to exert our newsrooms' influence ethically and prudently.

62. Except in their published writing, reporters, reviewers, critics and their editors in the arts may not help others to develop, market or promote artistic, literary or other creative ventures. They may not introduce artists to agents, publishers, producers or galleries; chefs to restaurant owners;

or designers to clothing manufacturers. They should refrain from unpublished commentary, even informal, on works in progress. They may not offer ideas or proposals to people who figure in their coverage or make investments in productions in their field. (Food writers and editors may not invest in restaurants.) They may not serve on advisory boards, awards juries or other panels organized by people who figure in coverage they provide, prepare or supervise. They may not accept awards from such panels.

63. An arts writer or editor who owns a work of exhibition quality (and thus has a financial stake in the artist's reputation) may arouse questions about the impartiality of critical judgments or editing decisions. Thus members of the feature staff who collect valuable art objects (paintings, photographs, sculpture, crafts and the like) must annually submit a list of their acquisitions and sales to newsroom management. If the top news executive falls under this provision, the list should be provided to the chief executive of the business unit.

64. Our company recognizes that its staffs include talented members who write books, music and plays; create sculpture and paintings; and give recitals. It also recognizes that a writer requires a publisher, a playwright a production company, an artist a gallery. Such relationships, however, can give rise to the fact or perception of favoritism. Staff members who enter into such arrangements must disclose them to newsroom management, and when appropriate the staff members may be disqualified from covering those with whom they have dealings.

Travel Journalism

65. No staff member of our company who prepares a travel article or broadcast — whether on assignment or

freelance, and whether for us or for others — may accept free or discounted services or preferential treatment from any element of the travel industry. This rule covers hotels, resorts, restaurants, tour operators, airlines, railways, cruise lines, rental car companies and tourist attractions. This prohibition does not rule out routinely awarded frequent-flier points.

66. Editors or producers who accept travel coverage from nonstaff contributors have an obligation to guard against real or perceived conflicts of interest. They should exercise care in assigning or editing freelancers who have accepted free services while working for other news organizations; such a reputation can embarrass us. We do not give travel assignments to anyone who represents travel suppliers or who works for a government tourist office or as a publicist of any sort. A newsroom manager may make rare exceptions for special purposes — for example, to assign a writer widely recognized as an expert in a particular culture. In such a case, the journalist's connections must be disclosed in the published or broadcast coverage.

67. Writers of travel articles must conceal their identity as journalists during the reporting, so that they will experience the same conditions as an ordinary consumer. If the affiliation becomes known, the writer must discuss with a newsroom manager whether the assignment can be salvaged. In special cases, the affiliation may be disclosed — for example, when a permit is required to enter a closed area.

68. No journalist may report for us about any travel service or product offered by a family member or close friend.

A6. Obligations to Our Company

69. The good name of our company and of our business

unit or publication does not belong to any of us. No one has a right to exploit it for private purposes.

70. Staff members may not use their company identification cards for purposes not connected with their work. ID cards may not be used to obtain special treatment or advantage from governmental, commercial or other organizations.

71. Staff members may not use company stationery, business cards, forms or other materials for any purpose except official business.

Speaking for the Company

72. Staff members must not disclose confidential information about the operations, policies or plans of our company or any of its divisions.

73. Senior news executives may authorize other staff members to comment publicly on policies or plans within the staff members' own areas of responsibility and expertise. If staff members are approached by outsiders or other media to discuss editorial content or policy more widely, our company policy requires that the caller be referred to the Corporate Communications department. Similarly, any inquiry addressed to a journalist about the company's advertising or other business activities should be referred to Corporate Communications.

74. Staff members are free to discuss their own activities in public, provided their comments do not create an impression that they lack journalistic impartiality or speak for the company.

75. Any staff member may respond openly and honestly to a reasonable inquiry from a reader about the staff member's work. If a reader asks for a correction, that

request must be passed promptly to a supervisor. If the request threatens legal action or appears to be from a lawyer, the complaint should be promptly referred to the legal department through a responsible newsroom manager.

Returning Borrowed Equipment

76. Staff members who borrow equipment, vehicles or other goods for evaluation or review must return them as soon as possible. Similarly, items borrowed to be photographed, such as fashion apparel or home furnishings, should be returned promptly.

77. Automobile reviewers should carry out their testing expeditiously and return the vehicle promptly. Any period longer than two or three days must be approved by a responsible newsroom manager. A reasonable amount of personal use is permissible if that use contributes to the review.

78. Staff members may keep for their own collections — but may not sell or copy — books, recordings, tapes, compact discs and computer programs sent to them for review. Such submissions are considered press releases. But no one may request extra copies of review materials for personal use. Local management may impose a ceiling on the value of review copies that journalists may retain. If not retained by the reviewer, recorded or digital media, such as tapes or disks, must be destroyed or returned to the provider; they may not be given away or left where they could be carried off for illicit copying.

79. Photographers, camera operators, picture editors, film editors, art directors, lab personnel and technology editors and reporters may not accept gifts of equipment, programs or materials from manufacturers or vendors. They may not endorse equipment, programs or materials,

or offer advice on product design. (This guideline is not meant to restrict our technical staff from working with vendors to improve our systems or equipment.)

A7. Advertisers and the Business Side

80. Our company and our local units treat advertisers as fairly and openly as they treat our audiences and news sources. The relationship between the company and advertisers rests on the understanding that news and advertising are separate — that those who deal with either one have distinct obligations and interests, and each group respects the other's professional responsibilities.

81. Journalists should maintain their independence by avoiding discussions of advertising needs, goals and problems except where those are directly related to the business of the newsroom. The news and advertising departments may properly confer on the layout and configuration of a newspaper (though not on specific content) or the timing of special sections, and on the timing and placement of commercials or Web advertising. The departments may also work together in designing new print, broadcast or Web offerings to make sure that the result is viable both journalistically and economically.

82. Advertising and "advertorials" (paid text or paid broadcast content) must not resemble news content. To the maximum extent permitted by local resources, advertorials should be prepared and produced by the business departments, outside the newsroom.

83. When authorized by top newsroom management, members of the news staff may take part in interdepartmental committees on problems that affect several departments, including news. As far as possible, the news representatives

should leave advertising issues to colleagues from the business side.

84. From time to time, when authorized by top news executives, journalists may take part in events organized by the company for marketing or promotion or investor presentations. But they should confine their role to discussion of our journalism and avoid the appearance or reality of making a sales presentation.

85. No one in our news departments (except when authorized by top news executives) may exchange information with the advertising department or with advertisers about the timing or content of advertising, the timing or content of news coverage or the assignment of staff or freelance news people.

B. On Our Own Time

B1. Participation in Public Life

86. The people of our company are family members and responsible citizens as well as journalists. Nothing in this policy is intended to abridge their right to live private lives — to educate their children, to worship and to take part in community affairs. But like other dedicated professionals, we knowingly accept disciplines — in our case, with the goal of ethical and impartial journalism.

87. As noted in Paragraph 7, some of these requirements apply to all newsroom and editorial page employees, journalists and support staff alike. No newsroom or editorial employee may do anything that damages our reputation for strict neutrality in reporting on politics and government. In particular, no one may wear campaign buttons or display any other sign of political partisanship while on the job while working for our company inside or outside the office. For all other purposes, "staff members" in this section

refers only to those who prepare or accept news content, as defined in Paragraph 5.

88. While the provisions of this document apply principally to journalists and some apply more widely to newsroom staffs (as explained in Paragraphs 5 through 8), the company recognizes that the activities of publishers and of their counterparts in broadcast and online operations — those senior executives to whom news and editorial department heads directly report — can also affect the appearance and reality of neutrality in reporting on politics and government. For that reason, Paragraphs 89 through 94 below will apply additionally to those executives.

Voting, Campaigns and Public Issues

89. Journalists do not take part in politics. While staff members are entitled to vote and to register in party primaries, they must do nothing that might raise questions about their professional neutrality or that of our news operations. In particular, they may not campaign for, demonstrate for, or endorse candidates, ballot causes or efforts to enact legislation. They may not wear campaign buttons or themselves display any other insignia of partisan politics.

90. Staff members may not themselves give money to any political candidate or election cause or raise money for one. Given the ease of Internet access to public records of campaign contributions, any political giving by a staff member would risk feeding a false impression that we are taking sides.

91. No staff member may seek public office anywhere. Seeking or serving in public office violates the professional detachment expected of a journalist. Active participation by one of our staff can sow a suspicion of favoritism in political coverage.

92. Staff members may not march or rally in support of public causes or movements or sign advertisements or petitions taking a position on public issues. They may not lend their names to campaigns, benefit dinners or similar events if doing so might reasonably raise doubts about their ability or their newsroom's ability to remain neutral in covering the news. Neighbors and other outsiders commonly see us as representatives of our institution.

93. Staff members may appear from time to time on local or national radio and television programs devoted to public affairs, but they should avoid expressing views that go beyond the news and analysis that could properly appear under their regular bylines. Op-Ed columnists and editorial writers enjoy more leeway than others in speaking publicly, because their business is expressing opinions. They should nevertheless choose carefully the forums in which they appear and protect the impartiality of our journalism.

94. A staff member with doubts about a proposed political activity should consult a responsible manager. These guidelines protect the heart of our mission as journalists. Where the conflict with our impartiality seems minimal, top news executives may consider matters case by case, but they should be exceedingly cautious before permitting an exception.

Serving the Community

95. Journalists should stand apart from institutions that make news. Staff members may not serve on government boards or commissions, paid or unpaid. They may not join boards of trustees, advisory committees or similar groups except those serving journalistic organizations or otherwise promoting journalism education. Depending on circumstances, newsroom heads may permit staff members

to serve on a board of trustees or visitors for a school, college or university, especially one with a family connection. Upon request, newsroom heads may also authorize a staff member to appear before a local school board to advocate decisions that may directly affect the journalist's children, but only if the issue falls outside the staff member's coverage responsibilities.

96. Our company respects community citizenship. Normally the restriction on joining trustee boards or advisory committees will not apply to local or neighborhood organizations that are unlikely to generate news of broader interest and those that do not generally seek to shape public policy. These typically include houses of worship, community charities, civic clubs, local libraries, fine arts groups, hobby groups, youth athletic leagues, country clubs and alumni groups. But news is unpredictable. Even neighborhood institutions sometimes find themselves in the spotlight. In that event, a staff member with ties to the institution must stand aside from any controversy and not take part in the coverage. In no case may a staff member's affiliation with our company be used to further the goals of such a nonprofit or volunteer organization.

97. Staff members may not solicit funds for social, political, religious or other philanthropic causes. Soliciting can create an expectation of a favor in return. Within reason staff members may help the groups described in Paragraph 96 with relatively modest fund-raising. They should never solicit anyone with whom they or their newsroom has professional dealings or invoke the name of our company or any of its units.

B2. Avoiding Conflicts Over Family

98. In a day when most families balance two careers,

the legitimate activities of household members and other relatives can sometimes create journalistic conflicts of interest or the appearance of conflicts. These can arise in civic or political life, professional work and financial activity. A spouse's or companion's campaign for public office would obviously create the appearance of conflict for a political reporter or television producer involved in election coverage. A brother or a daughter in a high-profile job on Wall Street might produce the appearance of conflict for a business reporter or editor.

99. Our company has no wish to intrude upon family members who are not its employees. Nothing in this document prohibits a spouse, companion or other relative of a staff member from taking part in any political, financial, commercial, religious or civic activity. Where restrictions are necessary, they fall on the company employee alone. But any attempt to conceal a staff member's activity by using a relative's name (or any other alias) would constitute a violation.

100. Staff members must be sensitive that direct political activity by their spouses, family or household members, such as running for office or managing a campaign — even while proper — may well create conflicts of interest or the appearance of conflicts. Even limited participation, like giving money or ringing doorbells, may stir suspicions of political bias if it becomes conspicuous. Staff members and their families should be wary of ambiguity. A bumper sticker on the family car or a campaign sign on the lawn may be misread as the journalist's, no manner who in the household actually placed it. When a spouse or companion makes a campaign contribution, it is wise to avoid writing the check on a joint account.

101. To avoid conflicts, staff members may not furnish, prepare or supervise news content about relatives, spouses or others with whom they have close personal relationships. For the same reasons, staff members should not recruit or directly supervise family members or close friends. Some exceptions are permissible — in a foreign bureau, for instance, where a married couple form a team, or in a small news department, with the approval of top newsroom management.

102. The company and its units depend on staff members to disclose potential problems in a timely fashion, with an eye to working together to head off embarrassment to all concerned. Any staff member who sees a potential for a conflict of interest in the activities of spouse, relatives or friends must discuss the situation with newsroom management. In many or even most cases, disclosure will suffice. But if newsroom management considers the problem serious, the staff member may have to withdraw from certain coverage. Sometimes an assignment may have to be modified or a beat changed.

B3. Protections Against Financial Conflicts

103. Every member of the company must be vigilant against any appearance of abusing nonpublic information for financial gain. That requirement applies to all departments.

104. No staff member may own stock or have any other financial interest, including a board membership, in a company, enterprise or industry about which she or he regularly furnishes, prepares or supervises coverage. This restriction extends beyond the business beat. A book editor may not invest in a publishing house, a health writer in a pharmaceutical company or a Pentagon reporter in a mutual fund specializing in defense stocks. "Stock," as used here,

means not just individual issues but also futures, options, rights, and speculative debt, as well as "sector" mutual funds (those focused on one industry).

105. In any region or locality where one company or industry is dominant, no news staff member likely to influence coverage of that business may own its shares. That description applies to top newsroom managers who are broadly responsible for coverage (including editorial-page editors); the head of each news or editorial department should decide to which rank-and-file journalists and middle-level editors it properly applies.

106. Staff members may not buy or sell securities or make other investments in anticipation of coming news coverage. Before trading, they must wait for a reasonable period, to give the public time to absorb the news. (Our legal department can advise on the timing.) This restriction does not apply to spot news reports that first appear on news agency wires or originate outside our organization.

Affirming Compliance

107. Staff members in each of our newsrooms should be asked, when hired, to affirm that they have no investments that would violate Paragraph 104 with respect to their proposed assignment. If a new staff member is unable to give that assurance, she or he must either dispose of the conflicting investment or accept an assignment where no such conflict exists. Similarly staff members should be asked, when hired, to affirm that to the best of their knowledge no household member or close relative has financial holdings that might reasonably raise doubts about the staff member's impartiality in the proposed assignment. Here, too, the answer could require recusal or an alternative assignment.

108. From time to time, management may ask staff members in any news or editorial department to affirm that they have no investments in violation of Paragraph 104. Such a request might be expected, for example, when a staff member is about to begin a new assignment or work on a particularly sensitive article. Similarly the journalist may be asked to affirm that to the best of his or her knowledge no household member or close relative has financial holdings that might reasonably raise doubts about the journalist's impartiality. If such conditions arise, the staff member must alert newsroom management.

109. If a journalist in any medium is assigned to provide or prepare coverage outside his or her own beat, about a company or industry in which she or he owns stock, the journalist must discuss the investment with the assigning editor or producer before beginning the work. Similarly, editors or producers assigned to extensive news coverage about companies or industries in which they have investments must advise their supervisors of potential conflicts before proceeding. In many instances it will be permissible for the work to go on, but a journalist who works on such an assignment may not buy or sell stock in the company or industry until two weeks after publication or broadcast.

Avoiding Market Conflicts

110. Journalists who regularly cover business and financial news may not play the market: that is, they may not conduct in-and-out trading, speculate in options or futures or sell securities short. Any of these actions could create an appearance of exploiting information not available to the public. Staff members who regularly cover business aspects of technology or other subjects are also subject to this rule.

111. Each newsroom is responsible for giving the public complete confidence that editors' choices are not biased by their personal finances. Depending on the editors' duties and on the volume, visibility and influence of each newsroom's business coverage, this assurance can be accomplished through periodic recusal, disclosure or an outright ban on owning stocks. Editors who regularly assign or supervise business or financial coverage would be well advised to avoid owning stocks in individual companies or sectors.

112. To avoid an appearance of conflict, business editors and their superiors in each news operation must affirm annually to their unit's chief financial officer that they have no financial holdings in violation of this set of rules. This requirement applies to editorial-page editors as well.

113. A staff member who owns stock and moves into an assignment where such holdings are not permitted must sell the stock. Each unit should devise a reasonable transition plan.

114. Whenever these rules require the sale of stockholdings, a staff member can satisfy the requirement by putting the holdings into a blind trust or the equivalent.

115. Though this document imposes some necessary limits on freedom to invest, it leaves a broad range of personal finance opportunities open to our journalists. Any staff member is free to own diversified mutual funds, money market funds and other diversified investments outside the staff member's day-to-day control. Any member may also own treasury bills, investment-grade municipal bonds, debt securities other than speculative bonds, and securities issued by The New York Times Company. And rank-and-file staff members are free to own stocks unrelated to their assignment.

B4. Freelance Writing and Broadcast Appearances

116. With approval of senior newsroom managers, staff members may accept freelance assignments that do not directly compete with our own offerings. Normally, work for competitors will not be permitted. In rare instances, permission may be granted when supervisory editors are not interested in the article or project offered by a staff member. Staff members are encouraged to offer their freelance work to their own news unit before trying to place it elsewhere.

117. Also with approval, staff members may participate in radio, television or online interviews or discussions, local or national, that deal with articles they have written or subjects that figure in coverage they provide, prepare or supervise. Such occasional appearances must not imply that the journalist speaks for our organization (unless that is officially the case). Staff members should ensure that the use of their names and their company affiliation, in materials promoting the appearances, is consistent with the newspaper's impartiality.

118. The senior executive of each news operation in the company, in consultation with that operation's top business manager, should maintain a list of the present and likely competitors in its journalistic arena. These might include any newspaper, magazine, television venture, online service or other medium, regardless of form, that has a similar editorial focus, either for a general audience or with particular segments of ours. If the competitive status of a freelance outlet is unclear, the staff member should consult with newsroom management.

119. Staff members may not appear on broadcasts that compete directly with our company's own offerings on television

or online. Otherwise they may make occasional broadcast or online appearances as outlined elsewhere in this document. But they must seek management's approval before accepting full-fledged assignments for reporting, anchoring, editing or production from any outside broadcast venture, even one that sells programming to us, buys it from us or makes it in partnership with us.

Governing Freelance Work

120. Staff members must ensure that their freelance work does not interfere with their normal responsibilities and that it is consistent with the policies and guidelines of this document and any standards adopted locally by our newsrooms.

121. Before accepting a freelance assignment, a staff member should make sure that the tone and content of the outlet are consistent with the standards of the local news department and our company. A staff member should place nothing elsewhere that implies sponsorship or endorsement by our company or its units.

122. In a radio, television, telephonic or online appearance, or any other public forum, we should avoid strident, theatrical vehicles that emphasize punditry or reckless opinionmongering. Our contributions should be marked by thoughtful and retrospective analysis. Generally a staff member should not say anything on the air or online that goes beyond the news and analysis that could properly appear under his or her regular byline.

123. Because outside work unavoidably reflects on our company, staff members who accept freelance assignments or make broadcast or online appearances should adhere to these guidelines in carrying out that work. For example, they may not accept compensation, expenses, discounts,

gifts or other inducements from a news source. Similarly, any staff member who establishes a personal site on the Web must insure that his or her online conduct conforms to these guidelines.

124. Frequency matters. Freelance work, whether in print or in electronic media, can create a conflict of interest if it is pursued with such regularity that it interferes with normal assignments or compromises the integrity or independence of the news report. Freelancing can also create a conflict if it identifies a staff member as closely with another publication, program or Web site as with his or her regular job. Writing under a pseudonym does not alter the obligation to comply with this provision.

125. A regular contribution to an outside enterprise may be permissible if it does not flow from the journalist's regular responsibilities or interfere with them, and if it does not involve content owed to our company and its audiences. Examples of acceptable affiliations might be a city editor who writes a monthly column on fishing or a news photographer who has a modest studio business. Staff members considering such continuing ventures should confer with newsroom management.

B5. Web Pages and Web Logs

126. Web pages and Web logs (the online personal journals known as blogs) present imaginative opportunities for personal expression and exciting new journalism. When created by our staff or published on our Web sites, they also require cautions, magnified by the Web's unlimited reach.

127. Personal journals that appear on our official Web sites are subject to the newsroom's standards of fairness, taste and legal propriety. Nothing may be published under

the name of our company or any of our units unless it has gone through an editing or moderating process.

128. If a staff member publishes a personal Web page or blog on a site outside our company's control, the staff member has a duty to make sure that the content is purely that: personal. Staff members who write blogs should generally avoid topics they cover professionally; failure to do so would invite a confusion of roles. No personal Web activity should imply the participation or endorsement of the Times Company or any of its units. No one may post text, audio or video created for a Times Company unit without obtaining appropriate permission.

129. Given the ease of Web searching, even a private journal by a staff member is likely to become associated in the audience's mind with the company's reputation. Thus blogs and Web pages created outside our facilities must nevertheless be temperate in tone, reflecting taste, decency and respect for the dignity and privacy of others. In such a forum, our staff members may chronicle their daily lives and may be irreverent, but should not defame or humiliate others. Their prose may be highly informal, even daring, but not shrill or intolerant. They may include photos or video but not offensive images. They may incorporate reflections on journalism, but they should not divulge private or confidential information obtained through their inside access to our newsroom or our Company.

130. Bloggers may write lively commentary on their preferences in food, music, sports or other avocations, but as journalists they must avoid taking stands on divisive public issues. A staff member's Web page that was outspoken on the abortion issue would violate our policy in exactly the same way as participation in a march or rally on the subject. A blog that takes a political stand is as far out of

bounds as a letter to the editor supporting or opposing a candidate. The definition of a divisive public issue will vary from one community to another; in case of doubt, staff members should consult local newsroom management.

131. A staff member's private Web page or blog must be independently produced. It should be free of advertising or sponsorship support from individuals or organizations whose coverage the staff member is likely to provide, prepare or supervise during working hours. Care should be taken in linking to any subject matter that would be off limits on the Web page itself.

B6. Books, and Rights to Our Materials

132. Any staff member intending to write a nonfiction book based on material that derives from his or her assignment or beat must notify newsroom management in advance. If the plan is to reproduce content created for any of our media, the Times Company owns that material outright. It may not be reproduced elsewhere without the prior written permission of the company. And it cannot be rewritten, updated or otherwise altered and then republished without the company's prior written permission. If a staff member is approached by someone seeking rights to Times Company material, the inquiry must be forwarded promptly to newsroom management.

133. Staff members who plan outside writing or other outside creative work must never permit an impression that they might benefit financially from the outcome of news events. Thus a staff member may not negotiate about rights to an article or story idea before the article has appeared. Staff members involved in covering a running story may not negotiate over creative works of any sort based on that coverage until the news has played out.

134. At no time may a staff member turn over notes, interviews, documents, outtakes or other working materials to any third party, including agents, producers, studios or outside production agencies, or share those materials with them unless legally compelled to do so. In case of such a request, the Times Company's legal department will provide assistance (consistent with collective bargaining agreements). As a matter of policy, the Times Company will not give commercial producers or publishers access to working materials any more than it would turn them over to government prosecutors for use in court.

135. Staff members offered consulting agreements in television or film by agents, producers, studios or others must consult a responsible newsroom manager before accepting. No staff member may serve as a consultant to a film or program that he or she knows in advance is tendentious or clearly distorts the underlying facts. In no case should a consulting role be described in a way that invokes our company or its local units, or implies our endorsement or participation.

C. Outside Contributors

136. Our audience applies exacting standards to all of our journalism. It does not normally distinguish between the work of staff members and that of outside freelancers. Thus as far as possible, freelance contributors to the Times Company's journalism, while not its employees, should accept the same ethical standards as staff members as a condition of their assignments for us. If they violate these standards, they should be denied further assignments.

137. Before being given an assignment, freelance contributors must sign a contract with the Times Company or one of its units. Such a contract obliges them to take care

to avoid conflicts of interests or the appearance of conflict. Specifically, in connection with their work for us, freelancers will not accept free transportation, free lodging, gifts, junkets, commissions or assignments from current or potential news sources. Independent broadcast producers, similarly, must comply with our ethical standards during their preparation of any news production that will bear the name of the Times Company or one of its units.

138. Assigning editors and producers who deal with nonstaff contributors should be aware that a freelancer's previous involvements and professional behavior can prove an embarrassment. They should make every effort to insure that a freelancer has no history or ties that would raise a real or apparent conflict of interest on a particular assignment.

139. The concise provisions of our freelance contracts cannot cover every circumstance that might arise. Assigning editors and producers should ensure that contributors are aware of this set of rules and to the greatest extent possible honor its provisions while on assignment for us. Any disagreement over whether a specific provision applies to outside contributors should be resolved ibefore the assignment proceeds.

Bibliography

Alexis Soloski, "The Plays What They Wrote: The Best Scripts Not Yet Mounted on a New York Stage", *The Village Voice*, May 21 - 27, 2003

Baase, S. "A Gift of Fire". PrentBaase, S. "A Gift of Fire". Prentice Hall, 3nd edition, 2008.

Beuttler, Bill. "Whatever Happened to the New Journalism?". BillBeuttler.com. http://billbeuttler.com/work50.htm. Retrieved on 2007-09-09.

Bowman, S. and Willis, C. "We Media: How Audiences are Shaping the Future of News and Information." 2003, *The Media Center at the American Press Institute.*

Denis Higgins. The Art of Writing Advertising : Conversations with Masters of the Craft: David Ogilvy, William Bernbach, Leo Burnett, Rosser Reeves, 2003.

Dvorkin, J.A. "Media Matters. Can Public Radio Journalism be Re-Invented?" January 27, 2005, *National Public Radio.*

Flew, Terry "New Media: An Introduction". Oxford University Press, Melbourne.

Fraser, Neil. "Theatre History Explained", *The Cowood Press*, 2004.

George, E. "Guest Writer Liz George of Baristanet Reviews Backfence.com Seven Months After Launch", 2005.

Glaser, M. "The New Voices: Hyperlocal Citizen Media

Sites Want You (to Write)!" November 17, 2004, *Online Journalism Review.*

Grubisich, T. "Grassroots journalism: Actual content vs. shining ideal." October 6, 2005, *USC Annenberg, Online Journalism Review.*

Herman, Edward and Noam Chomsky. 1988. *Manufacturing Consent: The Political Economy of the Mass Media.* New York: Pantheon.

Jack W. Plunkett. Plunkett's Retail Industry Almanac 2008: Retail Industry Market Research, Statistics, Trends & Leading Companies (December 2007), pp"416

Jessica Helfand. "What is graphic design?". *AIGA.* http://www.aiga.org/content.cfm/what-is-design. Retrieved 2009-06-29.

Jonson, Ben, *The Works of Ben Jonson*, Boston: Phillips, Sampson, and Co., 1853.

Just the Facts: How "Objectivity" Came to Define American Journalism, 1998.

Kaplan, Richard. *Politics and the American Press: The Rise of Objectivity, 1865-1920.* New York: Cambridge University Press, 2002.

Lasica, J. D. "What is Participatory Journalism?" 2003-08-07, *Online Journalism Review*, August 7, 2003.

Little Bill Clinton, *The Christian Science Monitor*'s serial following a year in the life of a young Congolese refugee.

Maher, V. "Citizen Journalism is Dead." New Media Lab, School of Journalism & Media Studies, Rhodes University, South Africa., 2005.

Mallory Stark and Martha Lagace. "John Irving's Lessons for Business". President and Fellows of Harvard College.

http://hbswk.hbs.edu/item/2000.html. Retrieved 2007-05-28.

Merritt, D. "News Media must regain vigor, courage." September 29, 2004, *PJNet Today*.

Meyer, E. P. "Public Journalism and the Problem of Objectivity." 1995, Published on personal website.

Mindich, David T. Z. *Just the Facts: How "Objectivity" Came to Define American Journalism.* New York: New York University Press, 1998.

Papandrea, Mary-Rose "Citizen Journalism and the Reporter's Privilege." *Boston College Law School (Minnesota Law Review, Vol. 91).* 2007. Retrieved on January 7, 2007.

Rosen, Jay "The People Formerly Known as the Audience," PressThink, June 27, 2006.

Schudson, Michael. *Discovering the News: A Social History of American Newspapers.* New York: Basic Books, 1978.

Schudson, Michael. "The Sociology of News Production." In *Social Meaning of News: A Text-Reader.* Dan Berkowitz, ed., 1997

Silverstein, Ken, "Turkmeniscam: How Washington Lobbyists Fought to Flack for a Stalinist Dictatorship", 2008.

Thompson, John. *The Media and Modernity.* Cambridge, Polity Press, 1995.

Index

H

●●●